ENTERING
THE MISSION OF GOD

FRAMEWORKS
FOR LAY LEADERSHIP

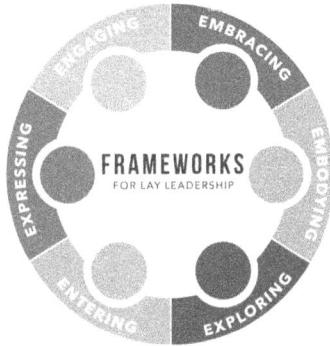

Rob A. Fringer, series editor

ENTERING
THE MISSION OF GOD

Richard Giesken

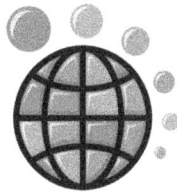

Global Nazarene Publications

ISBN 978-1-56344-889-8

Global Nazarene Publications
Lenexa, Kansas (USA)

Copyright © 2018
Richard Giesken

DIGITAL PRINTING

TABLE OF CONTENTS

Introduction to *Frameworks for Lay Leadership* 6

Foreword 7

Chapter 1: Introduction... 9

Chapter 2: Mission and God 11

Chapter 3: Mission and Humanity 19

Chapter 4: Mission and Culture 29

Chapter 5: Mission and Communication 37

Chapter 6: Mission and the Church 49

Chapter 7: Mission and Justice 59

Chapter 8: Mission and Holiness............................. 67

Chapter 9: Conclusion.. 75

Suggestions for Further Study................................. 77

Notes   79

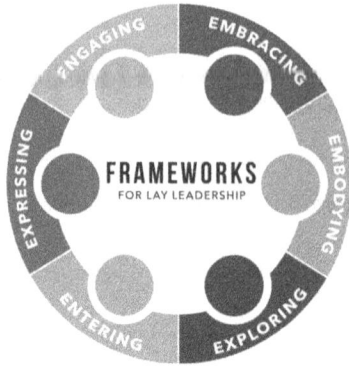

Scripture tells us that believers are "a royal priesthood" (1 Peter 2:9). This means that all Christians, in one form or another, are called into places of ministry and leadership. Not only is this a great privilege, it is also a great responsibility. Men and women desiring to serve in church leadership in some capacity undergo basic training to assure that they understand the foundations of the Christian faith and of our Nazarene identity. This includes a deepening knowledge and appreciation of Scripture, Theology, Ministry, Mission, History, and Holiness. *Frameworks for Lay Leadership* is a series of six books designed to do just that—equip lay leaders for ministry in the Church, whether local, district, or general. These books have the greatest impact when they are read, processed, applied, and contextualised in partnership with a qualified mentor.

Welcome to this journey of transformation!

ENGAGING THE STORY OF GOD
EXPLORING A WESLEYAN THEOLOGY
EMBODYING A THEOLOGY OF MINISTRY AND LEADERSHIP
ENTERING THE MISSION OF GOD
EXPRESSING A NAZARENE IDENTITY
EMBRACING A DOCTRINE OF HOLINESS

FOREWORD

Frameworks for Lay Leadership is a series of six books designed to equip laypeople in the Wesleyan-holiness tradition for ministry and leadership in a local church. The Church of the Nazarene defines a "church" as:

Any group
that meets regularly for spiritual nurture, worship, or instruction
at an announced time and place,
with an identified leader,
and aligned with the mission and message
of the Church of the Nazarene
can be recognized as a church
and reported as such for district and general church statistics.
(Nazarene Essentials)

This definition is grounded in biblical theology as well as the practice of the Early Church. Being a church should not be confined to a particular kind of building, or any building at all. Churches can meet at any time and at any place. In our context of the 21st Century, this definition of "church" should encourage and release laypeople to live out their own callings and gifts. That is to say, church leadership is not restricted to ordained clergy. From the beginning, God has used both women and men, young and old, educated and uneducated, rich and poor to carry out his mission in the world.

The Manual of the Church of the Nazarene (paragraphs 503-503.9) makes provision for qualified lay ministers, both male and female, to serve in ministerial leadership under the supervision of a pastor and church board or a district superintendent and district advisory board. However, before this can take place, lay ministers must clearly understand who we are, what we believe, and some of the practices that guide public ministry.

Nazarenes from the beginning have been known for theological tolerance. Two maxims capture this spirit, "In essentials, unity; in non-essentials, liberty; and in all things, charity" and "If your heart is as my heart, give me your hand." It is important, then, that lay ministers understand our core beliefs and distinctions (non-negotiables such as our theological understanding of God and scripture, our Wesleyan-holiness emphasis, and our ordination of women) as well as those areas where we may embrace various interpretations and opinions (such as the form of baptism, our understanding of how God created the universe, divine healing, the nature and timing of the Second Coming of Christ, and church structures).

Frameworks for Lay Leadership is designed to guide laypeople through a validated course of study in order to lead a variety of ministries in the Church of the Nazarene. This is particularly helpful in contexts where there are no ordained clergy to plant or lead new congregations or oversee existing ones. Upon completion of this course of study, under the guidance of an ordained Nazarene minister, a certificate of lay ministry may be issued by a local church board or a district advisory board.

John Moore
Regional Education/Clergy Development, Asia Pacific Region
Field Strategy Coordinator, Australia/New Zealand

CHAPTER 1

INTRODUCTION

There is a certain amount of romanticism surrounding the idea of mission. Many exciting and exotic tales of the missionary endeavours of David Livingstone, Adonirum Judson, Gladys Elwood, Harmon Schmelzenbach, and others have enthralled Christians for generations. For some, mission is part of the Christian DNA—it is an essential element of being the church. Although, only a special few people actually engage in the practice of overseas mission, the rest of the church stands behind them giving spiritual, administrative, and monetary support. For others, mission is part of a bygone colonial era, and they would prefer to focus their attention on the needs of their local community and neighbourhood. Finding a balance between these options is a challenge that needs to be addressed.

Wherever we stand on this issue, one thing is clear: mindless mission is dangerous. An adequate understanding of the foundation for mission is essential for the survival of the missionary cause and for the health of the church. Mission that is built on the foundations of personal enthusiasm, cultural superiority, romanticism, or denominational domination is bound to flounder and fail. Some seemingly pure motives for mission may prove to be less helpful than expected. An emphasis on individual conversion often narrows the reign of God to personal possession of the kingdom of God. The idea that mission is done to hasten the return of Christ focuses the life of the church too futuristically and misses the value of the current order of existence, which God has created and declared very good. Humanitarian motives for mission, on the other hand, easily equate economic development with success, while unwittingly sowing seeds of materialism and greed.[1]

The only adequate foundation and authority for Christian mission is Jesus himself. This may seem like an obvious and simplistic answer. However, upon deeper reflection, it proclaims Jesus as the embodiment of what God is doing and echoes his call to the church to be his body—his presence—in this world. By the witness of the Spirit, Jesus proclaimed the Kingdom of the Father and invited the church into his own life of mission.[2] From this perspective, the mission is entirely relational, expressing the purpose of the Triune God—Father, Son and Holy Spirit—to bring creation to fulfilment through an ongoing, dynamic, and sanctifying relationship. This is an intrinsic dimension of the Christian faith. The idea behind this book is that God initiates a redemptive mission to restore creation to its original purpose. People are the primary focus of this mission as well as the agents of God's initiative. As individuals are drawn into what God is doing in this world, communities of redemption and grace that reflect the character of God are established. God's kingdom, previously conceived as being out of this world and beyond this present age, is in Christ demonstrated to be already here. Justice and righteousness are its pillars, and its final consummation is described as a holy city which unites heaven and earth.

Entering the mission of God is intentionally engaging with the realities of the world today in all its diversity. It is not escapist idealism that pretends that all is well after repeating a magical formula. It is a life-transforming experience, empowered by the Holy Spirit, which works to bring this same transformation into every dark corner of the world, in order that there might be light once again.

DISCUSSION QUESTIONS

1. What is your vision of Christian mission?
2. How do the changing political realities of your local context and of the world affect how the mission of the church operates?
3. What are some of the barriers that keep people from entering the mission of God?

CHAPTER 2

MISSION AND GOD

In the beginning God spoke life into being (Genesis 1). The purpose of God was shaped into speech and took form in the material dimension as the words became our world. In that moment of creation, we see the very heart of God displayed. We are told that God is love (1 John 4:7-8); and we learn that love is creative and brings forth life. God demonstrates love by creating an environment in which humans may exist. God then forms the human from the ground of that very same environment, and God breathes life into the lump of human clay creating a living being who is intimately connected to God the creator (Genesis 2). "God, who needs nothing, loves into existence wholly superfluous creatures in order that He may love and perfect them."[3]

The relationship between God and humanity is reflected in the human relationship with creation. Placed in the garden, Adam and Eve displayed the life of God through their stewardship of the creation. With the nurturing life of God in the essence of their being, the dynamic relationship between God and humanity, and humanity and creation, brought into being a new manifestation of the love of God—the receiving and giving of life. Genesis 1–2 demonstrates this unfolding creative purpose of God as it describes the harmonious life between the first people, who were described as naked and yet unashamed. It paints a picture of the close relationship between the human beings and the Divine Being as they walked together in the cool of the evening. This intimate relationship between God and people manifested in harmony between people and environment, as the man and the woman partnered together to nurture nature forward in God's purpose.

The man and the woman were instructed to "fill the earth and subdue it" (Genesis 1:28). Unfortunately, this verse has too often been understood as power domination over nature—working to enslave the earth for human benefit. However, many biblical scholars argue that the original language carries the sense of tending and caring for creation in order to bring it to fullness. Some even declare caring for nature as the oldest profession in the world. As Adam and Eve begin their job, harmony and cooperation were to be the tools of their trade.

However, even a cursory glance across the world today reveals that there is a disharmony that has taken root in creation. Wars and ecological disasters, oppression and exploitation, are all reminders that the creation that was declared good in the beginning, is no longer so. The words of life that were spoken at the dawn of creation are being drowned out by the screams of hate and death. The very image of God that was forged deep in the human being (Genesis 1:26-27) is at best marred and distorted, and at times barely visible. The trustees of this world have become obsessed with their own grasp for power and desire to dominate and control by all possible means. The discord began with a questioning of the motives and purpose of God (cf. Genesis 3:1, 12) resulting in an act of distrust that brought with it fear, shame, and alienation from God and nature.

Through the ensuing chapters of Genesis 4–11 the echo of discord grew into murder and rebellion, fragmentation of society, and even the virtual destruction of humanity by the very environment they were supposed to subdue. Even after the flood, Noah, a righteous man who found favour with God, acted like a fool by indulging in a drunken display of reckless abandon (Genesis 9:20-25). At the end of Genesis 11 the purpose of God to bring fullness to the earth threatened to be stalled as people refused to fill the earth, but rather prefer to gather themselves around a towering monument to their own glory. The fear of being "scattered over the face of the whole earth" (Genesis 11:4) resulted in building a fortified safe space of unity and likeness, to the exclusion of others. Their intention was, as it were, to build a dam of God's blessing for themselves rather than an irrigation network for others. In the end, the very thing they feared befell them as God scattered them over the face of the whole earth.

Out of that scattering, the voice of God was heard by a man named Abram. A voice calling him to leave the comfort of his own people and the safety of his father's household to go to an unknown place.

The Bible is all about Mission

"Mission is what the Bible is all about."[4] It is not simply that the Bible supports mission, but that on each of its pages we see God at work to bring to completion that which was started in creation. God invited Abram (later named Abraham) into a relationship whereby he simultaneously entered into God's mission of redemption (Genesis 12:1-3). The rest of the Bible is an unfolding of Abraham's response to that invitation; it is a story of returning to God's heart. To enter into relationship with God is to enter into the mission of God and discover God's creative-redemptive purpose.

The sense of being a called people is central to the biblical community's identity. Even when Israel lost sight of the specifics of the mission, being a called or chosen people still shaped how they saw themselves. The life of this community was built around a response to God's *prevenient grace*—the grace of God that is positively active even before relationship is established. It is God who initiated both creation and redemption. In God's creative act life is given, and in God's redemptive mission life is being restored. Human beings are invited to respond to this act of grace by participating in and extending God's divine mission. The mission of God is not simply an activity of the church, but the action of God in this world to bring healing and restoration to creation, which is often referred to by the Latin phrase *missio Dei* – literally, the sending of God or the mission of God.

The Mission of God

The mission of God is to bring to fulfilment God's creative purpose through the plan of redemption, first through Israel and then through Jesus Christ. It is a continuation of God's prevenient grace that created life in the first instance, commissioned humanity to participate in bringing that life to fullness, and subsequently works to restore the dynamic relationship between God, humanity, and creation. The apostle Paul drew attention to this all-encompassing mission when he claimed that all creation groaned with longing to "be liberated from its bondage to decay and brought into the freedom and glory of the children of God" (Romans 8:21). Mission is not simply handing out a few tracts, or serving up Christmas lunch to the poor, or even proclaiming the gospel on a street corner. Mission does not always require crossing borders or learning a new language; mission is embodying the holiness and purpose of God as Jesus himself represented the mission of Israel.[5]

Embodying the holiness of God might conjure up visions of monastic communities or surreal expressions of bliss, but biblical holiness is far more practical as can be seen in passages such as Leviticus 19. The hallmarks of holiness are integrity, love, compassion, righteousness, and justice being displayed in personal and communal life. It should shape social life, family relationship, politics, economics, in fact, every aspect of life.[6] It is also simply not enough for individuals to possess a holy character. Fundamentally, holiness is communal; it is about our sharing life together in God. Therefore, we are invited to collectively participate in the mission of God.

Mission Is Not Just for Missionaries

The current human crisis, in all its brokenness and across all its cultural expressions, calls out for fullness. Wherever a human being exists, there exists the mission of God. There can be no separation of people's spiritual needs and physical needs. By extension, the missionary task of the church is too extensive for only an elite few to engage. It is necessary to include the whole church of God in the whole work of God and to recognise that "overseas missions" is not a separate division of the church.

Neither is the missionary task concluded with the proclamation of the gospel to a particular group of people. Until every knee bows and every tongue confesses Jesus is Lord (Philippians 2:10-11), and until these people are being discipled (Matthew 28:19-20), the mission is on!

There is a distinction between "mission" and "missions," which needs explanation. Mission (singular) is "God's self-revelation as the One who loves the world, God's involvement in and with the world, the nature and activity of God, which embraces both the church and the world, and in which the church is privileged to participate."[7] Missions (plural) was used in the past to designate the church's overseas outreach, and later to refer to outreach activities of the home church (so called "home-missions"), and has become synonymous with the "missionary ventures of the church," which are specific expressions of mission.

Recognising that the old paradigm of missions was focused "overseas," and missionary activity thought of as auxiliary to the work of the church, the term *missional* was coined in the early part of the 1980's to draw the whole Christian church into participating in the mission of God. A missional community is one that recognises that people are not saved out of this world to exist in a safe, religious bubble. Rather, they are sent back into the world as agents of God's kingdom. A missional church does not build towers of power in the hope that people will be attracted. The emphasis is on being salt and light in society, taking the initiative to testify to the resurrection of the Lord Jesus (Acts 4:33), and demonstrating God's grace through word and deed. It is not simply rebadging as *emerging, seeker-sensitive, social justice,* or *church growth.* These labels may be expressions of being missional, but they are only aspects of God's larger creative-redemptive purpose. Being missional is being fully engaged in God's world.

Long-Term Mission and Short-Term Missions

Being missional is all encompassing, but by necessity, it must be broken down into manageable parts. The church-in-mission is both a *sign* and a *sacrament*. A sign in that it points to something greater than itself (missions activity cannot encompass the whole of the mission of God but in some way manifest the incarnational love of God); a sacrament in that it serves to make real the reign of God in a specific time and place as a foretaste of the fulness of its coming. The church lives in the tension of "being called out of the world, and sent into the world."[8]

The phenomenon of short-term missions has become an integral part of many evangelical churches. Short-term is relative terminology for any "missions" trip from two weeks to two months to two years. It is estimated millions of Christians around the globe participate in these missions every year. Their "success" and effectiveness bears examination—is it genuine participation in mission or simply "missional tourism." Some negative aspects of short-term missions include: less than one in five short-term missions' groups engage with unreached people; three quarters of short-term missions are not done well; and financial expenditure on short-term missions could be more efficiently utilised.[9] These are not issues that should be lightly glossed over with platitudes that suggest these short-comings are justified by the hope that "just one person might be saved." Ignoring the potential damage of short-term, fly-in-fly-out missions is to jeopardise impact of the long-term mission. This is not to say that short-term missions have no value, but that they need to be planned and performed within the context of the long-term mission.

Roger Peterson identifies three key factors to consider in improving the impact of short-term missions. (1) Recognise, understand, and connect with God's already-at-work global purpose—leaders should realise they are not breaking new ground and thus tread carefully. (2) Respectfully partnering with local believers to develop ongoing relationship that grows the global mission—independent self-confidence is mostly hurtful and seldom helpful; therefore, plan and act cooperatively with seasoned time-tested mission agencies and national/local churches. (3) Genuinely engage in the global mission rather than using the short-term missions trip as experiences to further personal discipleship.[10]

By developing empowering partnerships with local congregations, positive results of short-term missions may outlast the short term. Utilising local knowledge to design the missions experience ensures that real needs are met while offering opportunities to experience participation in global mission. Comprehensive administration is needed to ensure effective use of resources, while qualified leadership and appropriate training allows for maximum impact. An aspect of missions that is often overlooked is thorough follow-up; reflection by participants allows for a consolidation of the experience and provides valuable learning upon which subsequent groups can build.

The essence of healthy missional engagement is maintaining the relational core of the *missio Dei*. When believers learn to follow the lead of the Holy Spirit in the ongoing work of God's creative-redemptive purpose, irrespective of geographical location, they are drawn into the global move of God. Where that engagement might take place may need specific skills, knowledge, and/or experience. Recognising what God is already doing in a place is essential to knowing one's own specific involvement. People do not have to cross an ocean to be involved in the mission of God. In fact, the beginning of mission has been said to start at the end of one's toes. A local missional perspective is essential to fulfilling God's calling—for wherever people end up will become local to them, and they will discover God already at work inviting them to participate in bringing to fullness what God has begun.

DISCUSSION QUESTIONS

1. How does the affirmation that "God is love" shape your understanding of creation and mission?

2. What is the purpose of the mission of God? What are some concrete ways that you and your local church can participate in that purpose?

3. What part does short-term missions play in the mission of God? What have you experienced as some of the benefits and drawbacks of short-term missions?

CHAPTER 3

MISSION AND HUMANITY

Being human is a complex reality, and science and religion appear to come at the issue from different angles. Arguments between the two tend to polarise people, leaving the middle ground very uncomfortable. To reduce humans to a purely physical existence that merely responds to sensory and environmental inputs seems to miss essential elements of humanness. That part of ourselves that appreciates beauty, utilises creative imagination to shape its surrounding environment, desires to express compassion, and has the self-awareness to know it is part of a bigger reality, cannot be defined by physics alone. In contrast, focusing solely on the human soul or spiritual dimension of being human ignores humanity's integral connection to the world around us.

Perceptions and Perspectives

Every day, people across the world navigate the intricacies of their societies with relative ease, thinking little about why they do the things they do. Generally, people do not wake up in the morning asking themselves: "Why do I exist? What is existence? How do I know what I know? Can I trust the people around me?" These "big" questions of life tend to be reserved for philosophers and day-dreamers. Still, people carry with them reasonably consistent assumptions (or beliefs) about life, the universe, and the people around them. Often these assumptions are unexamined and operate at a subconscious level, much like the operating system of a computer or smartphone. Only when something goes wrong and they face a situation that does not conform to their underlying understandings of reality do they begin to realise the complexities of being human.

These core assumptions develop over a lifetime as people interact with others, the environment, and the many circumstances of life. They become filters through which people interpret subsequent experiences, subconsciously guiding how they will respond to new situations. These ingrained perspectives shape the perception of life and inform the way people behave. Perceptions shape what is familiar and comfortable for people and regulate, to some extent, how willing they are to move beyond their comfort zone.

To be effective in mission, Christians must develop the capacity to reshape perceptions and gain an understanding of the perspectives and practices of the ones to whom they wish to communicate the gospel. Communication involves more than just speaking a language that the other person can understand. Even when a common language is used, misunderstanding can easily occur because of vast differences in the underlying cultures that have guided personal assumptions and beliefs about reality. In other words, sometimes people use the same words but are referring to completely different "dictionaries."

Understanding Worldviews

It is difficult to enter another person's world of experience, especially when that person is from a different culture to your own. It is not that others simply use a different labelling system, but that they attach deep meanings to objects and actions which in effect, create a whole new world. For one culture, a tree is simply a botanical reality, but for another it is the abode of evil spirits and a place to be feared and avoided. These different "worlds" are sometimes called *worldviews*. James Sire explores how differing worldviews create alternate realities for their subscribers. He notes that at the core of a worldview is a *commitment*. This commitment, he argues, is more than an idea that a person holds; it is part of the "central defining element of the human person."[11] In other words, worldview encompasses people's sense of identity, self-understanding, and how they perceive their relationship with the environment and other people around them. See Figure 1 for the eight basic building blocks of a worldview.[12]

EIGHT BUILDING BLOCKS OF WORLDVIEW

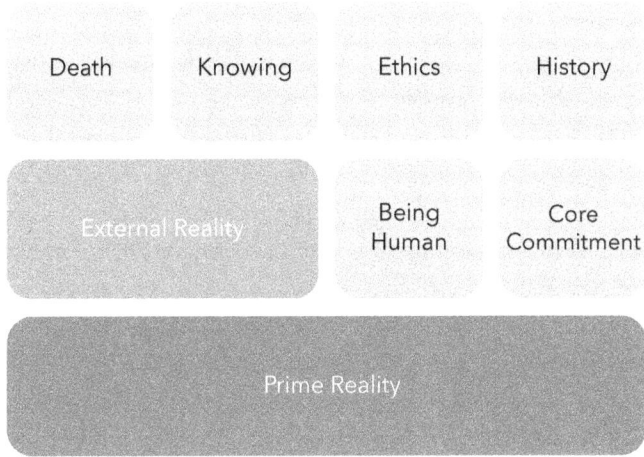

Death	Knowing	Ethics	History
External Reality		Being Human	Core Commitment
Prime Reality			

(FIGURE 1)

One's own answers to the questions of "what is really real?," "what is the nature of external reality?," "what does it mean to be human?," "what is the meaning of human history?," "what happens when people die?," "how does a person know right from wrong?," "how do people know anything?," and "what core commitment shape a person's answers?" may seem obvious and logical to one person, but complete nonsense to the next person. Naïve realism is the belief that everyone understands reality like I do. This naivety may give rise to blind spots, ethnocentrisms, or prejudices. Knowing that a person's worldview has developed over the span of his or her life as a response to personal experiences and interactions with others in a particular community may cultivate the understanding needed to communicate the gospel in ways to which that person can relate. Failure to recognise a person's worldview may result in miscommunication. It would be easy to mistake a person's superficial change in behaviour for a actual change of core commitment.

Boundaries, Borders, and Other Circles People Draw

Many Christians understand missions as crossing boundaries that separate "different worlds" to communicate the gospel of Jesus. These boundaries are often thought of as geographic, as in the traditional understanding of a missionary travelling to a distant country or "mission field." But the world today has become a global village where cross-cultural interactions are commonplace. Additionally, the understanding that certain countries are "Christian" appears to be fading. It can no longer be assumed that people living in the Western World are Christian. Increasingly the boundaries that need to be spanned are social, and the borders to be crossed are streets or neighbourhood divides. The church, the sent and sending community, needs to dismantle or circumvent the walls of fear and distrust often fuelled by media reports and political expedience by way of individual acts of trust-building.

Sitting at a table in a café, it is easy to become so engrossed in the conversation at this table and forget that there are other tables in the room, or for a moment become unaware that this is not the only café in the world. When people at your table are likable and saying things that are agreeable, it is hard to understand why those at the "other table" do not see things in the same way. Moving to a different table often means moving into a different conversation—if people do not take the time to listen to the conversation before speaking, their words may be completely irrelevant, no matter how important they may be. When crossing boundaries to share the good news about Jesus, it is important to first listen to those in this new circle. People need a context within which to receive new information and build new relationships. Seldom do people move to a point of decision to follow Christ without working through a process of discernment.

The "decision" to follow Christ is often referred to as *conversion* and involves a shift in core commitment. Core commitment, or ultimate allegiance, shapes people's worldviews and subsequently, how they behave. This change can also be described as a paradigm shift, without which, conversion will likely only be superficial—a conformity to religious rules without a transformation of the inner being. Eight important factors need to be understood about conversion:

1. Making disciples does not end with conversion. The goal of missions is not simply to get a person to say the "sinner's prayer." While this expression of faith in Christ might be helpful, it should not be seen as a magical formula which "converts" people into Christians. Faith is much deeper than one moment. It is a relationship that needs to be nurtured in order to grow. This nurturing most often happens in a community of people committed to growing in Christian holiness and maturity.

2. People will not begin to consider conversion until they are open to the need for change in their lives. From this realisation grows a recognition that such a change follows a radical shift at the very centre of their being—their core commitment.

3. At least some knowledge about the Gospel of Jesus is needed for people to shift their core commitment to Christ. People's knowledge, attitude, and intention in relation to the Gospel can be made explicit so as to facilitate journeying to a point of evaluating their relationship to Christ.

4. The *general revelation* of God (seeing God through creation) is attested to in Psalm 19. This "open letter" is understood as the beginning point of salvation. Curiosity to know more about God than is perceived in general leads people on a journey of discovery of the Creator.

5. From a Wesleyan perspective, God is already and always at work in the lives of all people, through the Holy Spirit, drawing them to repentance. This is also known as prevenient grace, "the grace that goes before." It is the starting point of saving knowledge. When people become aware of the stirring of God's grace in their lives and begin to respond, they open themselves to the possibilities of the means of God's saving and transforming grace.

6. While people may move toward the moment of salvation at different paces, there is almost always a progression as they become aware of the gospel and its significance.

7. General knowledge about the facts of the Gospel does not transform people until there is some "light bulb" moment concerning the implication of its truth for their lives in terms of their needs, motivations, and personal encounter with God.

8. The actual conversion of a person does not necessarily happen by way of a direct conscious decision, such as is made in a problem-solving exercise. Rather, the change of core commitment is a shift in foundational trust from one source of certainty to another—in the case of Christian conversion—trusting Christ. This is often facilitated through repentance, an expression of faith motivated by the Holy Spirit.[13]

The Conversion Process

If conversion is a tectonic shift in core commitment, then it can be considered a moment in a journey of discovering God. The conversion process can be described by using the Engel Scale, which measures a person's progress of faith formation (graphically portrayed in Figure 2). While the Engel Scale is represented as a linear progression, the reality is that it is often a journey with multiple detours and U-turns, and even after conversion there are moments of re-evaluation concerning the meaning of that moment.[14]

Conversion involves the whole person—including social, political, and economic.[15] When there is a shift in core commitment it is inevitable that this change will radiate to other areas of their lives as they continue responding to God's grace. This growth is thoroughly relational involving relationship to God, people, and environment. In changing those core relationships, conversion also changes people's orientation to what is right and wrong and what is just and fair as they are drawn into the creative-redemptive purpose of God. Conversion also includes how we use the resources at our disposal: money, time, talents, and so on. The Bible

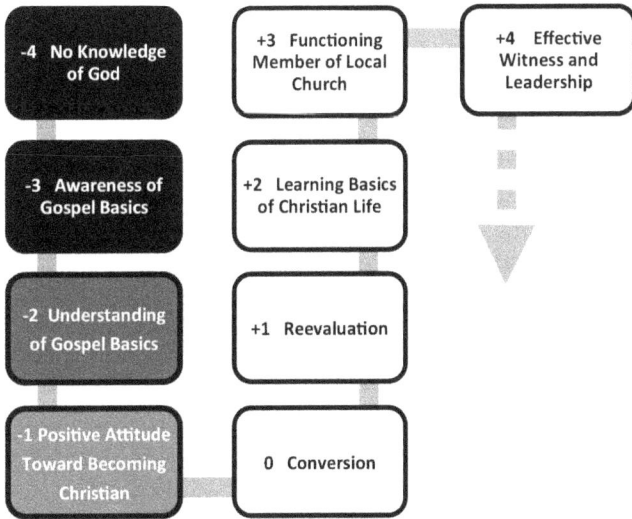

(FIGURE 2)

speaks in terms of "dying to self," and Paul declared that we "should no longer live for [ourselves] but for him who died for [us] and was raised again" (2 Corinthians 5:15).

It should also be noted that the Engel Scale does not have an end-point on the +plus end. A person never "arrives." The journey of faith for-mation in continuous throughout this earthly life. Growing in grace as a disciplined disciple works in the Christian a continual transformation into the image of Christ.

Building Community and Bridging Society

Humans are in essence communal beings. They are born in the company of others, raised in a "village," and celebrate milestones of life together with family and friends. Even in death people are usually buried along-side those of their community.[16] People often find their value in com-munity and shape their lives around communal values and expectations (both explicit and implicit). Community offers support, builds social bonds, and produces *social capital*.

Social capital can be thought of as the network of relationships that exist between individuals of a community. When these relationships are strong and functional, they may result in benefits beyond what individuals within the group could achieve on their own. These social gains increase community well-being. When individuals look beyond their own personal agendas to produce a benefit for the community social capital is built up. When people refuse to cooperate because of lack of trust and fear that their efforts will not be reciprocated or rewarded, their combined efforts are less than would be if they had entered into a partnership. This illustrates how community benefits the individual. Developing the relationships that produce social capital enables communities to achieve what they could not do individually. Likewise, communities of faith require trust and co-operation to be effective.

Social bonds are essential to the development of *cohesion* that builds the strength of the community. Cohesion refers to what binds the individuals in a community to each other. It facilitates trust, which is the glue that keeps individuals and communities together. Trust might be based on personal relationships, common goals, ideas or beliefs, or simply on geographic proximity. A common identity in Christ is the beginning point of the growth of a Christian community of faith.

While it is essential for a community to have social capital and cohesion to function effectively, it is also necessary for the church to build *bridging relationships* with the wider society in order to achieve the mission of God. Very often the resources needed to build these bridging relationships already exist among the people in the church. People within the church have pre-existing social relationships, family ties, and the ability to connect with those outside of the church. Without intentionally developing these bridging relationships, communication of the gospel will not move beyond the confines of the Christian community.

The social networks that build people into a church and enable the people of the church to bridge into the broader society are a natural part of being human. The social nature of human beings seeks out connections that develop into support networks that are essential to sustaining the individual. Through support, members in the community increase their own individual efforts, reinforcing the cohesion and building trust. The underlying structure of community is a web of relationships, upon which the social health of the community depends. When that web of relationships is built around healthy trust and valuing people, strong community is established. When this foundational human need for relationship is centred on Jesus as the embodiment of life, there is a profound potential for radical social transformation. Jesus demonstrated simultaneously who God was and what it meant to be human. His perspective on life was fully formed by his relationship in God. This subsequently informed his interaction with the people around him. Jesus's interests were directed by God's purpose while not detracting from his own freedom. In living his life for others, Jesus became the gravitational centre for a new kind of community. One that is based on love and co-operation rather than on competition and domination.

Not only did Jesus bind the community together, but he also laid down his life to become a bridge to others. An example of this is seen when Jesus intentionally crossed the boundary into Samaritan territory (John 4), placing himself in proximity to people who consciously demarcated themselves as "other." Jesus drew circles of inclusion that subsumed the circles of exclusion drawn by others. He modelled the mission of God by going to the rejected *and* the rejecting with the good news that the old barriers were not hindrances to God's purpose.

DISCUSSION QUESTIONS

1. What perceptions do you have about people from cultures other than your own? Have you become aware of any misperceptions that you have held about other cultures?

2. Looking at the "Eight Building Blocks of Worldview" (Figure 1), what specific things have shaped your own worldview?

3. What do you understand by the term "conversion"? Can you outline your own "process" of conversion? What insights from the Engel scale can you apply to your conversations with people?

4. How do you get people to trust you? How do you know who you can trust?

5. What kinds of things has your church done to build *bridging relationships* with the wider society in order to achieve the mission of God? What additional things can you be doing?

CHAPTER 4

MISSION AND CULTURE

"Mission is about proclaiming a holistic gospel of the kingdom of God in the tradition of Jesus."[17] In proclaiming the gospel, it is important that the message be understood by the hearers. Communication theory recognises that there are many potential barriers to getting the message across, one of them being cultural differences. These differences may be overt and obvious, such as language, customs, or social space. Others may be more covert and confusing, such as people's beliefs, values, and feelings. These elements are often rooted deep within people and their cultural worldview, hidden from sight yet producing visible signs of their presence.

Barriers to communication are not one-sided. They exist in both the receiver (or receptor) as well as the proclaimer of the gospel. Every person who seeks to share the story of God's salvation in Christ unwittingly filters the story through his or her own cultural perspective and personal experiences. Being aware of the influence of cultural structures may help shape communication in a way that minimise these barriers. Understanding a worldview is key to this type of communication, since it is at the heart of a culture.

What Is Culture?

Culture may be thought of as "the collective programming of the human mind that distinguishes one group or category of people from another."[18] The definition may apply to different levels of society. There may be a national or ethnic culture, which defines many people under one umbrella. Also, within that larger group, there may be any number of subcultures that represent interest groups, business corporations, local communities, and even specific family groups. The implication from this perspective is that cross-cultural mission does not have to travel vast distances to engage with a different culture.

THE DYNAMICS OF CULTURE

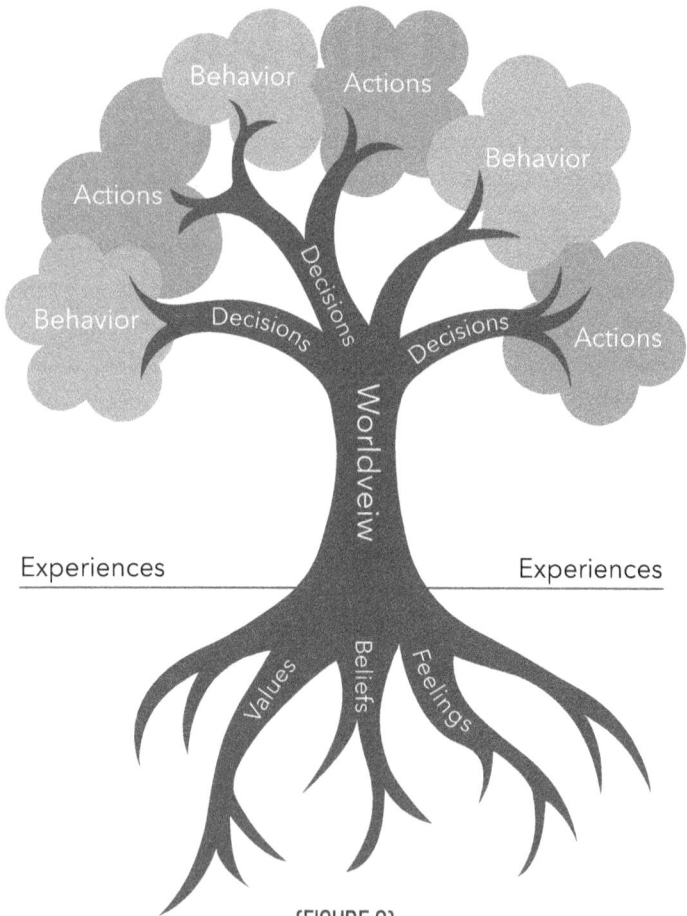

Behavior Actions Behavior Actions Behavior Decisions Decisions Actions Worldveiw Experiences Experiences Values Beliefs Feelings

(FIGURE 3)

Understanding that worldview is at the core of culture, it is possible to see how it defines what a person or group of people assume to be real. This then shapes how they evaluate what is true, what is good, and what is enjoyable. These beliefs and values are like the roots of a tree, hidden from sight but defining what is seen above the ground. These hidden elements of culture will manifest themselves visibly in the way people dress, behave, and how they share and receive information (see Figure 3 for The Dynamics of Culture[19]). It may be relatively easy to change outward expressions of human behaviour, but until the gospel shapes people's worldview, their true beliefs and values will remain mostly intact. In the metaphor of the tree—unless the life-giving water of the gospel soaks into the ground in which the tree is planted, and the roots soak up its nutrients—the leaves will wither, and the fruit will fail.

Cross-Cultural Capacity

People's effectiveness in mission will be directly related to their ability to bridge the cultural differences between themselves and the people to which they are reaching out. When missionary pioneer James Hudson Taylor arrived in China, most missionaries of the time lived in western enclaves and maintained their western lifestyles. Recognising this as a barrier to the gospel, Taylor learned the local language, adopted the national dress, moved out of the mission compound into the community, and communicated in ways that his audience could relate. The result was an overwhelming response to the gospel and a legacy that continues to impact the region for Christ a hundred years later. Taylor's innovation was so successful that he has been recognised as one of the most influential missionaries ever. His influence in China was greater than almost any other foreigner of his time, both secular and spiritual.[20]

Taylor and others, who are effective in cross-cultural settings, display what could be described as *cultural intelligence*, which is defined as the capacity to function effectively in culturally diverse situations.[21] Obviously, it is important to understand the cultural context of the new environment, but moreover, bearers of the gospel also need to be aware of their own cultural biases. Three significant factors may help develop the cultural intelligence needed for this task.[22] First, *information* about the new culture. While information alone does not produce capacity, it is instrumental in providing the necessary framework within which to grow. Second, *motivation* to learn. Where there is a significant drive towards connecting with a culture, capacity to adapt is increased. Third, appropriate *action* within the norms of the new culture. This is the ability to behave in an appropriate way and assimilate to the new culture. While these three factors can be mastered, individual personality plays a significant part in how successful integration into the culture will be. Being open to new cultures is a significant ingredient in effective cross-cultural mission. Openness means a willingness to be uncomfortable so as to begin and sustain relationships across cultures.[23]

Jesus provided us with an incarnational model of mission (cf. John 1:14), which should serve as a paradigm for all mission effort. Jesus "emptied himself, taking the form of a slave" (Philippians 2:7, NRSV) as he entered our human culture to bring salvation. He "did not come to be served, but to serve, and to give his life as a ransom for many" (Mark 10:45). To communicate the gospel effectively, *humbling* and *entering* are essential parts of the openness necessary to build trust and identification with people in a cross-cultural setting. Humbling and entering are also vital in trying to assure that personal cultural values do not become confused with authentic expressions of the values of the kingdom of God in a new cultural context.

Trust and Compromise

Contextualised mission can be dangerous if the core message of Christ is compromised. Relating the gospel to a different culture, runs the risk of using inappropriate metaphors or words to illustrate the gospel. For example, in the context of some cultures where vines are destructive weeds, being a part of "the vine" of Christ may communicate something very different from its intended meaning. Some local practices are so deeply engrained that they may distort the gospel if used as a way of bringing understanding to that culture. No culture is neutral, and every culture has elements that are both positive and negative. To allow cultural practices to undermine the essential nature of the gospel is known as *syncretism*—a blending of incompatible, local beliefs with foundational Christian beliefs and practices.

Developing relationships of openness and trust are essential for working through these issues with local followers and potential followers of Jesus. What is necessary is for people who enter relationship with God through Christ to be guided by the Holy Spirit to discern what is culturally and theologically appropriate. Imposing external cultural norms may simply replace one set of bad values with another. Introducing Christ to a culture is like introducing two people to each other and allowing them the freedom to define their own relationship. Where elements of the local culture positively support the mission of God, they can be encouraged and integrated into the life of the church.

Dealing with Culture Shock

Adjustments to living or working in a new cultural environment can be physically and emotionally overwhelming, this is called cultural shock. No matter how well prepared a person may be, culture shock can still have a significant impact on the cross-cultural worker. The loss of familiar cultural reference points produces the same experiences as when faced with threats that destabilise a person's sense of security. For many people, this produces anxiety that may manifest in different ways. Being aware of the stages of cultural adjustment can help minimise the impact of culture shock and establish a new normal within which to flourish.

While every situation is at least somewhat unique, experts have identified four stages commonly experienced by people moving into a new cultural environment:[24]

STAGE 1: *Excitement* – The person experiences a holiday feeling with all the excitement, new sounds, sights, smells. There is an initial and superficial tourist-like involvement in the host culture. The similarities and differences between the new culture and home culture are fascinating. Every new experience seems like an opportunity to learn.

STAGE 2: *Withdrawal* – As the novelty of the new environment begins to wear off, focus shifts toward the differences between the new culture and home culture. Small differences seem magnified and anxiety levels increase, which leads to a diminished capacity to deal with the ordinary aspects of life. Stereotypes and prejudices begin to surface. The local people suddenly seem hostile and unpredictable, leading to a withdrawal from interaction with locals, and a gravitation to people from home culture. Homesickness is intense, and every experience of the new culture is reminder of how much you miss friends, family, and the familiarity of home.

STAGE 3: *Adjustment* – New routines begin to introduce a feeling of familiarity, and the logic and values of the new culture begin to make sense. Cultural cues become easier to read, and feelings of isolation begin to fade. Elements of the new culture begin to be appreciated and a sense of humour begins to return. Deeper cultural learning begins to take place as an openness to new perspectives develops.

STAGE 4: *Biculturalism* – The "new" culture is no longer new, and the person feels "at home." A realism allows for a balanced critique of the new culture with some aspects embraced wholeheartedly, even in preference to home culture. Certain patterns of behaviour from the new culture become instinctive and the person can function effectively in the context of their new life.

These stages are not always a straight forward path. The process of cultural adjustment is subject to several factors. It is often more cyclical than linear. People going through cultural adjustment may find themselves at different times and in different situations returning to a previous stage of culture shock, especially when confronted with new stresses in the host culture. Over time familiarity and the ability to function with the new cultural context establishes a level of competence from which the gospel can be shared.

DISCUSSION QUESTIONS

1. How would you define culture? What levels of cultural difference have you encountered through life and/or travels?

2. What would you identify as your own culture's top three values and/or beliefs? What cultural stories have shaped your church's identity?

3. How would you go about discovering new information about a culture that is different to your own? What makes some people more

open to other cultures? What "cultural mistakes" have you observed from people who are foreign to your culture? Which mistakes have made you laugh; which mistakes have offended you? What have you learned from "cultural mistakes" that you have made?

4. How can Jesus's "emptying" of himself inform mission activity in a cross-cultural context?

5. Have you experienced cultural shock? What can a person do to prepare for culture shock?

CHAPTER 5

MISSION AND COMMUNICATION

Language is a curious thing. There are over 7,000 languages spoken in the world today, of which only 150–200 are used by the bulk of the world's population. Ninety percent of languages are used by groups of less than 100,000 people, and we know of forty-six languages that are spoken by just a single user. Not all languages are equal—English has about 250,000 distinct words, while the Sran language of Suriname contains only 340 words. Almost all languages use similar grammatical structures, even if they use different words and alphabets, of which there are forty-six to choose from. Every language is a symbolic expression of thought, working to connect two minds.

Models of Communication

Humans are communicative beings. There does not seem to be a moment that people are not communicating. This reality has escalated recently with the advent of technological advances and new ways of harnessing those technologies. Technically, communication is a process in which a message is encoded into a set of symbols by a transmitter. That message is then sent via a specific channel or media to a receiver that decodes the message. In that process, "noise" might interfere with the transmission

THE COMMUNICATION PROCESS

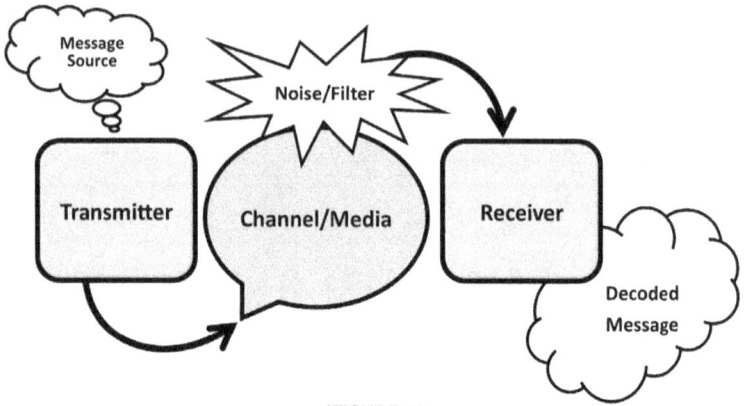

(FIGURE 4)

of the message. This standard model of communication is graphically displayed in Figure 4.

When a transmitter wants to communicate an idea, he or she must first formulate the idea. That idea needs to be coded into words or symbols that make sense to the transmitter. Those symbols may take shape in the form of spoken words or written symbols. But the coding may also take on a non-verbal aspect (or coding) that is displayed in the transmitter's behaviours or expressions. The encoded message is then sent via a channel or media such as a mobile phone voice or text message, face to face chat, piece of paper, or any other format the transmitter has at his or her disposal. Any interference with the transmission of the message is referred to as noise. This can be anything from actual noise preventing the receiver from hearing the message, psychological noise such as the emotional state of the receiver when the message is sent, or even the attitude the receiver has toward the sender. Once the receiver has the message, the task of decoding begins, which can be relatively easy if the receiver uses a similar coding system. However, untransmitted assumptions made during the encoding of the message, or a range of "filters" such as cultural background, level of education, or personal prejudice, may result in miscommunication. Ideally, feedback from receiver to transmitter can determine if the message has been correctly understood, or if there is need for clarification.

This simplification of the model of communication highlights the potential for failure in communication at any point in the process. In cross-cultural communication, the assumed encoding symbols are often not the same, and many of the untransmitted assumptions embedded in the worldviews of both transmitter and receiver might be unfamiliar to the other. For effective communication to occur a common understanding and strategy of encoding needs to be developed. The most efficient way to develop such common understanding is to enter the world of the other to discover their assumptions and decoding strategies and use their paradigm to communicate your message. This is what God did in Christ.

The Gospel is Person

While there is much talk about postmodernism, most westerners, including most Christians, live within a Modern worldview. Their perspective on life is shaped by ideas developed during the Renaissance and 17th century Enlightenment. These ideas tend to emphasise rationality, logic, and analytical thinking. Technological advances of the past twenty years have added an extra layer of complexity to this worldview. These factors shape the perception and performance of mission. Approaching mission with a Modern mindset has the potential to reduce the gospel to facts and figures, logically constructed arguments to prove the truth (aka facts), and strategies based on rational analysis of utilitarian goals.

But there is a mismatch between the Modern worldview and biblical worldview. The worldview of the Bible does not seem consumed with proving facts and propositional statements about intellectual belief. Rather, it draws meaning from a faith position that God entered human history and interacted with this world in a significant way.[25] If the Bible is all about mission, then mission is our primary source for understanding the gospel. This understanding comes to fulfilment in Jesus. He is the pre-eminent expression of God's interaction with humanity. He is the embodiment of the mission of God. The gospel is a person.

There are several stories told from different parts of the world about statues of Jesus where the hands have been broken off. Whether by bombing raids in Germany or England during the second world war, or vandalism in San Diego, or police brutality in Soweto, the disfigured image of Jesus stands as a reminder of the invitation to embody Christ by being his hands today. Where hurting hearts and needy lives cry out, the poem attributed to Teresa of Avila continues to serve as a call to mission:

Christ has no body but yours,
No hands, no feet on earth but yours,
Yours are the eyes with which he looks
Compassion on this world,
Yours are the feet with which he walks to do good,
Yours are the hands, with which he blesses all the world.
Yours are the hands, yours are the feet,
Yours are the eyes, you are his body.
Christ has no body now but yours,
No hands, no feet on earth but yours,
Yours are the eyes with which he looks
compassion on this world.
Christ has no body now on earth but yours.

The words of Jesus still ring out, "As the Father has sent me, I am sending you" (John 20:21). What may be missed in the English translation is that the "you" in Greek is plural. The mission of God is communal, not individual. While individuals participate in the mission, they do not have their own "missions." No football team exists with just one member. Although the striker may receive the spotlight and the adulation, it would be impossible to win a game without the support of the rest of the team. And the team embodies the hopes and dreams of an even larger community who participates and identify with it. A missional community is people who understand that inward transformation is a journey that manifests in outward transformation. It does not end when a person enters the community. The community and the transformation are not the goal, it is only the beginning.[26]

Words and Actions

God enters into relationship with people to bring to fulfilment the purpose of creation. Relationship is connecting and communicating. While general revelation testifies to the existence of God, Christians affirm that God has especially been revealed through the witness of the faithful community as recorded in the Bible, and specifically through the person of Jesus Christ. The Christian mission is not simply content to propagate information *about* God but exists to draw people into relationship *with* God by embodying the purpose of God. Communication is about both words and actions—the one is not understood without the other.

While it is important to communicate the content of the gospel, it is also vital to demonstrate the content through practical expressions of God's love and concern for people and creation. Information alone does not transform lives. Only 7% of meaning in communication is derived from spoken words; a further 38% is derived from the way those words are spoken, and 55% of meaning comes from facial expression.[27] This illustrates that communication is as much, if not more, about building relationships than about transmitting information. How communication takes place is important because it shapes and filters what is communicated. It is easy to create unintended barriers through body language and tone of voice. For example, standing with arms folded saying "I love you" communicates something quite different to the same words accompanied by a warm embrace.

The importance of relational embodiment of the gospel is even more necessary in a cross-cultural setting, since so many of the non-verbal cues that people use are not necessarily trans-cultural. For some a smile might intend to communicate sincerity and friendliness, but to a person of a different culture, that smile may be interpreted as devious and fiendish. Likewise, a touch to the arm of the other may be construed as a violation of their person, rather than as an extension of trust. Strong relationships can transcend many of these cultural faux-pas and provide a safe learning space for the cultural novice.

Trust

Trust is the fabric of relationship. Until trust is established with a person or a group of people, communication will be severely limited at best and possibly completely rejected, regardless of whether or not the message is true. In the world today, there are significant barriers to trust that need to be addressed before gaining a hearing of the gospel. Misinformation and efforts to discredit the church make it all the more important to develop a context of trust within which to proclaim the gospel of Jesus.

Trust has several key ingredients. First, trust takes *time*. There is no schedule for building trust because each relationship is unique. Second, building trust involves a certain amount of *risk*. There is a bilateral vulnerability that needs to be navigated before trust can flow. The initiator of relationship takes the first step in vulnerability. As with verbal communication, the language of trust is not universal and needs to be communicated in a way that will be understood by the other person. It is imperative to understand trust building from their perspective. Third, trust is not automatic, it needs to be *nurtured*. Proximity produces possibilities—shared experiences and conversations are rich nutrients with which to grow trust. Finally, generous portions of *forgiveness* may be needed from both parties to eventually foster a significant foundation of trust for relationship and gospel communication to flourish.[28]

Jesus demonstrated an incredible capacity to communicate the heart of God's love to people. In many of the Gospel narratives it is surprising how quickly people entrusted themselves to Jesus. When Jesus encountered people, he welcomed them into his presence—blind beggars, little children, sinners, and untouchables alike were not judged nor were the socio-cultural barriers an obstacle for him. Without excusing their behaviour or minimising their brokenness, Jesus demonstrated trustworthiness, and from that place of trust flowed a transformational encounter that demonstrated the focus of the mission of God to establish fulness of life according to John 10:10. To believe in Jesus is to trust him.

Seven Dimension of Cross-Cultural Communication

Significant differences between two or more cultures is referred to as *cultural distance*, which can be a significant disruptor of cross-cultural communication. Jesus embodied God's commitment to humanity by entering human existence, thereby reducing the cultural distance between heaven and earth. In doing so he communicated the heart of God by demonstrating effectiveness across seven key areas which impact how the gospel messages is encoded, transmitted, and subsequently received.[29]

Ways of perceiving – Everyone has perspectives through which they understand the world around them. Very few people stop to consider how they think about the world, even fewer take the time to try see the world through the eyes of the other. People interpret the actions and events around them to make sense of their environment and construct a perceptual world that conforms to their understanding. In the Gospel accounts of Jesus's encounters with the other, Jesus was fully present as he engaged them in conversation. The Samaritan woman at the well declared that Jesus told her everything she had ever done (John 4:29); he saw her from her perspective. When Jesus was introduced to Nathaniel he declared "Here truly is an Israelite in whom there is no deceit" (John 1:47); he saw into the depth of the person. Entering into the world of the others, listening carefully, and learning from them facilitates effectively communication.

Ways of thinking – People across the globe are born with similar cognitive abilities. Those abilities are then shaped by the social setting and learning opportunities available to them. The social context teaches people how to think about the environment, and how to decide what is beneficial and what is not. Some social contexts evaluate whether or not something is beneficial based more on the individual, while others place greater emphasis on the group. As creatures of habit, people tend to follow the patterns of thought familiar to them. To direct people to a new destination, an understanding of their mind map (way of thinking) and their points of reference is essential. When Nicodemus sought Jesus out one night, Jesus drew him a new map—"I tell you, no one can see the kingdom of God unless they are born again" (John 3:3). Nicodemus's response indicated that he did not possess the same roadmap that Jesus was using. When Jesus clarified the route, Nicodemus seemed none the wiser; apparently the reference point that Jesus was using did not make sense to him. So, Jesus used an account from the Old Testament, about Moses lifting up a snake in the wilderness—an illustration that may leave many modern readers a bit lost, but for Nicodemus this was a familiar road marker—which directed his journey to the discovery of a new way of thinking.

Ways of expressing ideas – Language embodies cultural priorities. For example, the Himba people of Namibia do not have words for blue and green. They live in a dessert environment where it may not be important to distinguish between these two colours. As a further indication of the importance of expressing ideas, studies done with Himba children indicated that given a selection of colours, they were unable to distinguish between blue and green colour swatches. Researchers found that as "children started learning their cultures' colour terms, the link between colour memory and colour language increased."[30] Without words to express ideas, ideas fade and cease to exist. Jesus used parables as a powerful way to breathe life to ideas in a way that transcended specific words. When asked to clarify the word neighbour, Jesus told the parable of the good Samaritan (Luke 10:25-37); when confronted with why he socialised with people of dubious character, Jesus told three parables about lost things (Luke 15:1-31). Jesus did not simply teach people lessons, he expanded their vocabulary and extended their experience of God's grace.

Ways of acting – People tend to conform to the behaviour patterns of those around them. Generally, societies develop accepted norms for what is considered appropriate behaviour. Failure to meet those expectations can have dramatic effects. What may be considered acceptable in one culture may be considered rude in another. Navigating through the cultural norms of a new situation may feel like crossing an ocean without a chart, never knowing when you are going to run aground. Cross-cultural workers are full of stories of embarrassing situations where they have used a hand gesture or made a sound that caused dismay. Often these situations produce much laughter and can be chalked up as a learning experience. Occasionally, though, their actions had more dire conse-quences. The thousands of ways a person "ought" to behave, be it how to give and receive gifts, when to stand or sit, knowing who should walk in front or behind, and who may hold hands with whom, are learned infor-mally as people grow up in their own culture. While cultural guides may point out some well-known customs, countless others will have to be learned through trial and error—a good sense of humour is helpful. The ministry of Jesus is interesting in this regard, because he often broke the cultural taboos and did the "wrong thing," be it eating with unwashed hands or healing a person on a holy day. Jesus's actions were never arbi-trary. When he broke the "rules" he did so to draw attention to a deeper human need. Where the religious leaders were trying to control people's behaviour, Jesus was looking to liberate people by connecting them to the source of life.

Ways of interacting – Social structures define appropriate interac-tions. Some societies have very hierarchical structures where there is a very clear understanding of how younger members may interact with the older generation, or how people of the opposite sex may interact in public. Other societies are far more casual in this regard, but have different expectations regarding bribery or communal use of property. Western societies tend to be more individually orientated, while much of the rest of the world has a more community orientation. Entering a different social structuring may cause discomfort and awkwardness, but any attempt to intentionally operate from an ethnocentric (focused on one's own culture) perspective will cause confusion and even intense dis-comfort in the other. This may create cultural barriers which could have been avoided. Where possible it is better to absorb that discomfort and to set the other at ease, this can open an audience for the proclamation of the gospel. Jesus showed great sensitivity to the social structures of culture where they benefited clear communication. Jesus equally showed the power to challenge and transform oppressive social structures: he touched lepers who were considered ceremonially unclean; he spoke to women in public; and he rebuked the disciples for trying to turn the children away. Jesus communicated utmost care and compassion for the people he encountered, speaking words of life to them. He embodied positive transformational values—values that said, "people matter; love is primary; and the marginalised are included."

Ways of channelling the message – The ways that a message is communicated greatly impact how it is received. Written forms are sometimes less effective than oral presentations, and audio-visual materials may lock in unintended cultural perceptions. The concept that the medium is the message[31] implies that the chosen way of communication affects how the message will be perceived. The medium can be thought of as the "container" in which the message will be sent. The communicator needs to consider carefully both the content of the gospel presentation as well as the ways of channelling the message, since the medium tends to become embedded in the message. In recent years communication technology itself has impacted the social norms of various societies. When the gospel is introduced to an oral culture via the medium of print, something of the rich imagination required for oral transmission is lost as the message is reduced to paper. In the western world, the decline in functional literacy and a shift to digital medium and "sound bites" are dramatically changing the effectiveness of traditional ways of transmitting the gospel. One example of this is how the use of social media has redefined the meaning of friendship, appreciation of beauty, and boundaries of community. Jesus is both the message and the medium. He is the way that God ultimately communicates love, but he is also the content of God's message. In Jesus the message is firmly embedded in humanity not simply as an abstract idea, but as a tangible expression of God. Any attempt to disentangle Jesus and his message reduces both beyond comprehension.

Ways of deciding – The logic behind how people make decisions is based on a complex set of interactions within their value system, which has been shaped in part by their culture. While everyone knows what it means to make a decision, few are aware of the processes involved in deciding. This is also true for when an individual "makes a decision for Christ." In communal societies the individual does not perceive himself or herself as indivisible from the community and therefore will be reluctant to take action that is not consistent with the will of the community.

Those from individualist societies, on the other hand, tend to make decisions based on personal preference or perceived gain. Additionally, the methods of processing information for decisions differ between literate and oral communities and weight of duty and responsibility impacts the process in a variety of ways. Logical conclusions of philosophical arguments do not work equally across cultures and often emotional appeals trump reason. Furthermore, life-changing decisions are seldom made in isolation from a thousand lesser decisions, which build up over time. Readers are often impressed by the early disciples' willingness to leave their jobs on the spot to follow Jesus. While this appears to be the case, the reader has no knowledge of the prior relationship between Jesus and those he initially called to follow him. Nor do most western readers understand the kinship structures that existed to build trust in relationships based on family allegiances rather than on the individual's capabilities. Jesus was a master of relationship and demonstrated this in all his dealings with people. Never manipulating, nor allowing himself to be manipulated, Jesus made himself vulnerable to others by way of invitation. Not everyone of Jesus's day accepted his invitation, but none were excluded from Jesus's challenge to respond to the clear communication of God among them.

The story of the tower of Babel tells how humanity's quest to establish its own security resulted in a total collapse in their ability to communicate with each other (Genesis 11:1-9). The text states that God "confused" their language (verse 7). But language is only part of the art of communication. The willingness to hear the other and the compassion to understand can transcend the language barrier. In Jesus, God reunites humanity despite their languages, and through the Holy Spirit God pours compassion and mercy into the human soul to build a kingdom of priests—people who will bridge the divide between each other for God's glory. In Jesus the message of God is experienced and fulfilled.

DISCUSSION QUESTIONS

1. What cultural "noise" are you aware of when trying to communicate the Gospel? What forms/media of Gospel presentation are most

popular in your own culture? How have those forms potentially distorted the Gospel?

2. Where do you see your church engaging in "mission as information"? What is the danger of this approach? How can this be avoided? Can the gospel be separated from culture?

3. Which of the "Seven Dimensions of Cross-cultural Communication" do you think is most important? Why?

CHAPTER 6

MISSION AND THE CHURCH

Any discussion about mission would be incomplete without exploring the meaning of the word itself. Derived from the Latin verb *mittere* meaning "to send," mission is used to describe the church's response to God's calling to be active in the purpose of God in this world. The term *missiology* is used to label the study of Christian mission. The scope of that study, however, goes far beyond merely reflecting on the history of the church's endeavours to make it to the ends of the earth, and by necessity draws together diverse disciplines such as theology, biblical studies, organisational leadership, communication theory, cultural anthropology, intercultural studies, study of world religions and culture, psychology, and sociology—not to mention other vehicles for mission such as agricultural sciences, education, health care, and almost any form of human activity and social interaction. Missiology is all-encompassing!

Sending and Gathering

"When everything is mission, nothing is mission," is an often-quoted warning not to lose sight of the purpose of Christian mission to participate in fulfilling the creative-redemptive purpose of God. When people engage in Christian mission, they share in and extend the Father's sending of the Son, and the Father's and Son's sending of the Spirit.[32] The church is the community gathered around Jesus, not simply as spectators of his life, but as participators in his mission. Before his ascension

Jesus commissioned his disciples to continue what he had started. The disciples' task was not just to talk about Jesus in a historic sense, but to embody God's Spirit as a fresh representation of God's presence and purpose in the world. Thus, *missio Dei* is God's sending to establish a people in every culture, who are to be the foundation and model of a new humanity.[33]

While the word mission is rooted in the principle of being sent, it would be a misunderstanding of the nature of that mission to emphasise the "going" to the detriment of the "gathering." The New Testament word for the church is *ecclesia*, meaning "gathering." The mission of the church is not simply to "go," but to "make disciples." Christian salvation is ecclesial, meaning it is connected to "being the church." To be formed by the Holy Spirit into a new way of being community, one which engages in passionate and life-transforming worship, radical forgiveness and sharing of resources, and practicing a hospitality that invites others to participate in God's holiness, is the most evangelistic thing that the church can do.[34] The early church's proclamation of the gospel was not just words but powerful acts of grace (Acts 4:32-35).

Social Holiness

A Wesleyan understanding of the mission of God can be derived from John Wesley's idea of social holiness. This phrase is often misunderstood as a call to acts of social justice. What Wesley was pointing towards is the reality that a life of faith is seldom effectively lived in isolation. Christian faith seeks community.

This raises two important implications for a missional church. The first is that the most effective environment within which Christians grow in grace is a community of faith. Wesley's idea of social holiness captures the notion of graced fellowship, where people experience a fuller knowledge of God in Christ together. When grace is actively and intentionally received, it has a transformative effect.[35] Through sharing together in various means of grace, the Spirit forms in the disciple the image of Christ.

The second implication is that this "life together" is itself not isolated from the general society. Social holiness inevitably seeks to connect God's transforming love experienced within the community of grace with those who have not yet received it as such.[36] It constantly explores ways to include outsiders. This seems to be a clear application of the words of Jesus to love God with all your heart, soul, mind and strength, but also to love your neighbour as yourself (Mark 12:30-31). While for some the mission of the church is to "seek and to save the lost" (Luke 19:10), this was never intended to happen without drawing people back into the community of grace where the love of God is embodied, for salvation is not simply a guaranteed entrance into heaven, but the transformation of the person into the character of Christ, and an inclusion into the new community.

Increasing Circles of Inclusion

"Who is my neighbour?" is the question that prompted Jesus's parable of the good Samaritan (Luke 10:25-37). Jesus challenged his hearers to broaden their categories of thought. They were thinking that "neighbour" meant people from their own community. Circles of inclusion are often drawn very tight. It is very easy to remain in a comfort zone with likeminded people. This behaviour is often manifesting fear of the unknown and a desire to control circumstances. When people intentionally refuse to enter into grace-filled relationships, seeking out only those with whom they are comfortable, they are inadvertently attempting to "control" the gospel. These decisions in effect decide who should receive grace and who should not. Building relationships beyond comfortable circles of friends is a way of re-enacting this parable of Jesus.[37]

There is a strong emphasis on inclusion in the biblical narrative. From the presence of non-Hebrews in the Exodus from Egypt (Exodus 12:38), to the inclusion of Rahab and her family into the people of Israel (Joshua 6:25), and the heart-warming confession of fealty by Ruth the Moabite (Ruth 1:16), the biblical community of faith has welcomed "the other" into the circle of inclusion. This reflects an important aspect of the nature of God; he is the one who calls the newly formed nation of Israel to love the foreigner in their midst (Leviticus 19:34) and who includes enemies in the plan of salvation (Romans 5:10).

Sharing God's love with others should never be a means to an end. To do so is to diminish the value of the "target of our affection." People are not pieces in a cosmic chess game, to be manipulated, manoeuvred, and sacrificed. Jesus's parable of the sheep and the goats (Matthew 25:31–46) illustrates that genuine embodiment of the transforming love of God in the life of a disciple flows naturally to others, not as an obligation to law or duty, but as an expression of love for God in Christ.

Saved to Serve

The Apostle Paul often referred to himself as a *slave* or *servant* of Christ (e.g., Romans 1:1; 1 Corinthians 4:1; Galatians 1:10). Ministry in the Bible is typically described as service. Being missional is more than just speaking the gospel; it is living the gospel in service to God and others. This does not imply a works righteousness—trying to earn salvation. It is the experience of God's grace that brings freedom, expressed as union with God's mission to bring freedom to all. Cross-cultural servanthood is a model that embodies this principle. The framework for this model is an understanding that relationship is foundational to all ministry and serving is intended to empower others through encounter with Jesus.

Serving is not popular in a world of entitlement and power politics. The very thought of the word servant conjures up images of oppression and dishonour, yet Jesus equated this lowly position with greatness in the kingdom of God (Matthew 20:25-28). Serving is great because it reflects the self-giving love of God. Acting for the benefit and betterment of others is one of the chief characteristics of love as outlined in 1 Corinthians 13. This is no sentimental definition of love, but a dynamic expression of the fulfilment of God's creative-redemptive purpose. Serving is not a sideshow in a three-ring circus, it is the manifestation of God's love in this life.

The ability to connect with people in a way that values them for who they are and empowers them to live God-glorifying lives is the very definition of serving. A model for *servanthood mission* can be built around five interlocking principles each of which facilitates deeper love for God and neighbour.[38] The first is *openness*, which is crucial for the growth of any mission. Prevenient grace prepares the possibilities for those who are willing to follow. Openness to what the Spirit of God is doing leads to service. This openness is first and foremost directed toward people and growth in relationship. A missional church will be welcoming to all whom it encounters, both in the sending and in the gathering. Proximity produces possibilities.

The second principle of servanthood mission is *acceptance*. A missional church seeks to communicate the value and worth of others. This does not mean that everything that a person does will be condoned, but acceptance does boldly proclaim that nothing can separate us from the love of God that is in Christ (Romans 8:31-39). It can be said that belonging precedes believing. Serving that is not rooted in the acceptance of the other will be perceived as shallow or patronising and will have little transformative value. Transformation is one of the primary purposes in redemption—to be transformed by the renewing of the mind and be formed to the character of Christ (Romans 12:1-2; 8:29). Grace does not transform from afar and proximity will only happen through openness and acceptance.

Trust is the third principle of the servanthood model for being a missional church. This is the ability to establish strong connections where there is assurance that the other will act in positive ways and not intentionally harm the relationship. It is the fabric of relationship, both personal and communal. Openness and acceptance will facilitate trust, but relationships need to be nurtured personally. This is done more effectively around a dinner table or BBQ than in church programs and seminars. Individuals and cultures express and build trust differently. There is no formula that is without risk, but without trust the missional church will simply remain an unrealised dream.

Because the missional model attempts to address specific needs rather than pepper the world with platitudes, the fourth principle is *learning*. Without learning, mission easily becomes simple promotion of a personal agenda. To be truly contextual in ministry an understanding of the culture is essential. It is easy to read about people and cultures, and this is an important part in the learning process. However, individuals rarely fit the stereotypes, and a "one size fits all" mission program will seldom meet the real needs of people. An outsider's perspective will always be biased, thus there is a need to learn from those you seek to serve. But the insider also has certain biases and blind spots; this situation requires a journey of mutual discovery and learning. The ensuing conversation is bound to produce new perspectives which expand the knowledge of all involved.

The fifth principle of the model is *understanding*—being able to interpret patterns of behaviour accurately to reveal the values and integrity that lie behind. Almost no one holds values that they believe to be wrong. Most people maintain a worldview built on their understanding of the world. Being able to enter into the worldview of another enables the servant to recognise the values that underpin observed behaviours and distinguish between cultural adaptations and gospel essentials. The goal is not to conform the world to a specific culture, but to allow God's

CROSS-CULTURAL SERVING MODEL[39]

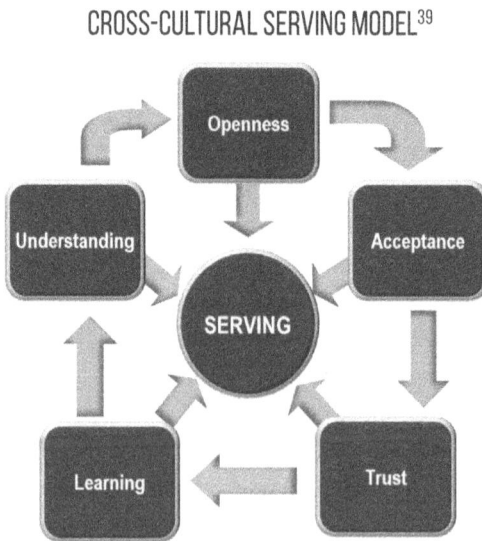

Openness

Acceptance

Understanding

SERVING

Learning

Trust

(FIGURE 5)

kingdom to manifest in all cultures. Understanding creates the opportunity to serve intelligently and avoid confusion or damage.

Every element of this model works to facilitate the growth of relationship and the capacity to empower others. Although each principle builds sequentially upon the other, they also function dynamically between each other (see Figure 5). Mission seldom occurs in a neat three-point plan. New understanding can facilitate greater acceptance, which in turn opens the participants to deeper learning and heightened levels of trust. Genuine empowering servanthood often generates reciprocal service, which when graciously received becomes the cornerstone of healthy community and a beautiful expression of the kingdom of God in action.

Church in Context

Churches around the globe are discovering that there is no perfect program or formula for doing church. Communities are more diverse than ever before, and the world is more interconnected than at any other time in history. *Globalisation*, which primarily refers to international economic integration, also describes the flow of ideas, culture, and economic resources around the globe. Modern transport and international cooperation has facilitated large-scale cross border movements of people. It is not unusual to see a person of African birth enjoying Mexican food in Brisbane's "Chinatown." And yet the taste of that Mexican food and even the items on the menu would probably not be quite the same as it would be in downtown Mexico City.

As international companies export their products and ideas around the globe, they recognise that what works well in one place does not have the same effect in another. This has given rise to *glocalisation*—taking a foreign product and adapting it to a local context. Thus, rice and spaghetti can be found on the menu at McDonald's in the Philippines, and beetroot on the burgers in Australia. Whenever there is an international interaction of cultures, there is an inevitable change on both sides. The age of discovery saw European powers spread their influence around the globe. They also experienced a reciprocal return flow of people, ideas, and cultural influences.

There needs to be a form of glocalisation in global mission. Styles of music, forms of liturgy, leadership structures, even length of sermons (or messages), and the design of buildings should reflect the culture of the people they seek to serve. Both the form and the function of the church should reflect the relational realities of the context it finds itself in, while preserving the essence of the Gospel. The function of the church is to connect people to Christ in a way that establishes the kingdom of God in their midst. The form reflects the context of the people as they express their relationship with Christ in creative ways. The term *contextualisation* is used to describe this process.

Contextualisation is not just repeating formulas from far away fields or bygone eras with a slightly local tweak. It seeks to identify signs of God's already active presence[40] and to embed the gospel in the culture. It is addressing the actual needs of real people by discovering what salvation means for them in their context. People are only able to respond to the gospel when it makes sense to them. People are not saved by abstract philosophical constructs, but by recognising and responding to the presence of Christ inviting them to follow him. Christ in context makes sense.

Just as there are many layers to culture, so there can be many layers to the contextualisation of the Gospel. A popular tool for describing these layers is the so-called "C1-C6 Spectrum."[41] Originated in the context of mission in the Muslim world, C1-C6 offers insights that may be applied cross-culturally. It describes six types of Christ-centred communities, each focused on worshipping Jesus as Lord and holding to the central teachings of the gospel. However, each community expresses that Christ-centred identity in increasingly cultural ways through use of local language, customs, and music styles. Each subsequent level of the spectrum embeds the Gospel deeper into the local context and needs, and away from the dominant expressions of the Christian faith. The six "communities" are differentiated as follows:

C1—Traditional Church using "Church" Language: This is a generic form of Christianity considered "traditional" church. It often reflects Western culture and perpetuates a cultural chasm between the church and the surrounding community. It could also reflect regional traditional Christian churches such as the Egyptian Coptic church, Syriac Christianity, or a number of other ancient forms of the church. Believers openly call themselves "Christians" and use traditional terminology that requires insider Christian knowledge or learning to understand.

C2—Traditional Church using "Contextual" Language: Essentially the same as C1 except for language. Though local language is used, religious vocabulary is probably still distinctively Christian. The cultural gap between society and C2 is still large. Often more "converts" are found in C2 than C1.

C3—Christ-centred Communities shaped by Local Culture, using "Contextual" Language and Religiously Neutral Insider Cultural Forms: Religiously neutral forms may include folk/cultural music, ethnic dress, artwork, non-Christian religious elements; these might be reinterpreted and used as purely cultural forms of worship. The aim is to reduce foreignness of the gospel and the church by conforming to biblically permissible cultural forms. People might meet in a church building or more religiously neutral location. C3 congregations are comprised mainly of converts and still identified distinctly as Christian.

C4—Indigenous Christ-centred Communities using "Contextual" Language and Biblically Permissible Cultural and indigenous religious forms: Like C3, but, biblically permissible indigenous religious forms and practices are also utilised (e.g. praying with raised hands, observing fasting, avoiding certain foods, abstaining from alcohol, using ethno-religious terms, dress, etc.). C1 and C2 forms avoided. Meetings are not held in church buildings and almost entirely comprised of "converts." C4 believers, though highly contextualised, are usually identified as distinct from the non-Christian community. They identify themselves as "followers of Jesus" (or something similar to avoid the term Christian).

C5—Christ-centred "Messianic" Communities who have Accepted Jesus as Lord and Saviour: Believers remain legally and socially within the host community. Somewhat like the Messianic Jewish movement. While aspects of indigenous theology that are incompatible with the Bible are rejected, efforts are made to express the Christian faith in terminology that is reinterpreted from the surrounding culture and religion. Participation in corporate non-Christian indigenous worship varies from person to person and group to group. C5 believers meet regularly with other C5 believers and share their faith openly with the surrounding society. Locals may see C5 believers as part of the community.

C6—Small Christ-centred Communities of Secret or Underground Believers: Due to fear, isolation, or threat of extreme governmental/community legal action or retaliation (including death), C6 believers worship Christ secretly (individually or perhaps infrequently in small clusters). They are usually silent about their faith and are virtually indistinct from the surrounding community.

Persecution necessitates the secretive nature of C6 but does not silence the witness of the Spirit of God in their lives. Throughout history the church in various places has faced extreme levels of persecution and has found a way to survive. Being distinguishable from the surrounding culture is not a prerequisite for being a Christian, but living in obedience to Jesus as Lord is. It is not the place of outsiders to dictate how God's people should act in these contexts, but to support through prayer and confidence that the Spirit of God is able to guide and lead as clearly in every context the church finds itself.

DISCUSSION QUESTIONS

1. Does your church focus on "gathering" or "sending"? How can you keep a balance between these two movements of the church?
2. What needs do you see in your community? What resources do you have that might meet these needs?
3. How can servanthood mission be applied in your local context? What unintentional barriers to openness can you identify in your church? How is your church seeking to be an accepting community? How did Jesus demonstrate acceptance without compromising his mission?
4. What doe trust look like in your culture? How have you seen people from other cultures expressing trust? What are some of the risks of trust? How can those risks be managed without stifling relationship?
5. What are some aspects of the life of your church that are more cultural preferences rather than gospel essentials?

CHAPTER 7

MISSION AND JUSTICE

John Wesley believed the mission of the church was "to reform the nation and ... to spread scriptural holiness over the land."[42] This vision looked to move the church of his day beyond being a religious pastime to engaging a broken society to bring it to wholeness and to fulfil the purpose of God in creation. The idea of social transformation has roots in the Old Testament prophets who declared that God was renewing all things (e.g., Isaiah 43:18). The purpose of Jesus's own mission is described in 1 John 3:8 as "to destroy the devil's work." The mission of God brings liberation from the bondage of sin, which eats like a cancer at the fabric of society. The New Testament concludes with visions of a new heaven and a new earth (Revelation 21:5), inviting the reader to enter into its reality. Righteousness and justice are the pillars of the mission of God. The gospel of Jesus is not escapism. This world is worth saving and the church is the anticipation of the restoring reign of God.

Social Engagement and Transformation

When the Bible uses the word *justice,* it usually addresses vital areas of human and divine concern and draws a picture of *what ought to be.*[43] It is action to make things right. For Wesley, justice, mercy, and truth are the summary of the moral attributes of God. They are an expression of the image of God in which human beings are created and to which humanity is being restored in Christ.[44] Justice for the vulnerable is one of the chief concerns of the biblical prophets as they call Israel to re-engage with the mission to which God has called them. Biblical justice is more about acting on behalf of the vulnerable and powerless than about dispensing punishment to those who offend God.[45]

At the foot of Mount Sinai, the earliest missional community, the nation of Israel, was given a law code which established justice as one of the central values of the community. The identity of the people of Israel was founded in their experience of liberation from Egypt. Their affirmation of faith was that God saw their oppression, heard their cry, and acted in compassion. They discover that freedom did not mean reckless abandon to the whims of the flesh, which led to a slavery of a different kind. They were free to be something more—a community of righteousness and justice, reflecting the character of God who saved them. Biblical faith resists the urge to spiritualise religion out of the realm of social engagement and individual responsibility. Such an approach is contrary to faith in the God who is first encountered as the divine deliverer of the oppressed.[46] The mission of God engages real life situations. It is not simply a call to Sunday worship. Without confronting systems of injustice, religious faith becomes escapism.

In the early church, if someone had a need, others "sold property and possessions to give to anyone who had need" (Acts 2:45). This radical generosity saw no division between spiritual and physical need. Poverty and oppression were understood as an assault on God's intended purpose in creation.[47] This same understanding outlawed lending money for profit in the community. While a church may not be able to rewrite the rules of the world financial system, it may be able to meet the needs around it, and refuse to become consumed by the materialism and consumerism or the world. Jesus spoke more about financial matters than about heaven or hell. Perhaps it was in recognition that for many the possession of money seemed like heaven and the lack of it felt like hell. The relationship between money and power is obvious, and the need to be freed from such power even more so.

In his own embodiment of the mission of God, Jesus confronted injustice. Matthew 5 is a manifesto of the mission, the constitution of the New Covenant. The beatitudes are a reminder to those who are *not* "blessed" that God is at work in the world not only to reverse their fortunes, but to completely transform their environment. They are also a call to the hearer (or reader) to embrace these values as a way of personal and social transformation. Jesus not only taught the beatitudes, he lived the beatitudes. His life confronted our culture with the words "[God's] kingdom come, [God's] will be done, on earth as it is in heaven" (Matthew 6:10).

Christ and Culture

Confronted with the relationship between the church and the surrounding culture, theologian Richard Niebuhr described five approaches toward missional engagement with the world:[48]

1. *Christ against Culture.* In this approach Christians are called to separate themselves from the surrounding culture, assuming that it is unredeemable. The church is seen as the antithesis of the world, and the mission is seen as preparing people for heaven and standing against this evil world. Converts are called to make a radical break with their past to save their souls. Nature and people are regarded negatively, and redemption is framed as escape from this reality.

2. *Christ and Culture in Paradox.* Here Christians live in the surrounding culture and avoid its negative aspect as best they can. There is a recognition that by necessity there is some engagement in the corrupt worldly system in order to survive materially. The physical and material reality of this world is minimised because the focus is on being "spiritual"—waiting for the ultimate reality of a spiritual heaven.

3. *Christ of Culture.* This position sees history as the unfolding work of the Holy Spirit. It recognises godly values in human culture, even where Christ is not acknowledged. Some speak of "anonymous Christians"—people who are responding to the prevenient grace of God within their own cultural/religious traditions. It affirms that all truth is God's truth and has an optimistic view of people and nature. The mission of the church is seen as proclaiming God, who is already active in the culture.

4. *Christ above Culture.* From this perspective culture is seen as basically good but distorted by sin; thus, the mission of the church is to build towards a higher culture. There is no rejection of the surrounding culture and the church works alongside the culture to reconcile the world to God and bring all under the rule of Christ.

5. *Christ transforming Culture.* Here again culture is regarded as essentially good, but corrupted by sin. The mission of the church is to affirm the good in human culture and reclaim what has been corrupted by sin. This view takes the position that eternal life begins in this life as people are introduced to Christ and changed to be like him.

Niebuhr acknowledged that each of these approaches were flawed because the fulness of faith had not yet been established. This suggests that any human effort to establish the kingdom of God is thus flawed. Perhaps this is because humans are ever intertwined with their own effort to manipulate the natural and social environment to suit their own needs. Thus, people can only be agents of the kingdom of God to the extent that the kingdom is formed in them (individually and collectively). "Kingdom mission flows directly out of the kingdom story,"[49] which means that it is people focused. The church is not the Kingdom, but the overlap is far greater than most recognise. The same King governs the Church and the Kingdom; the same laws apply to the Church and the Kingdom; and the same power of redemption is at work in the Church and the Kingdom.[50] The life that is centred on Christ must surely be transformed and work towards God's creative-redemptive purpose. The five models of social engagement are not airtight, nor do they describe all the possible ways God works in the world. Sometimes God confronts, sometimes God encourages. God always calls people higher towards the transformation of all of creation to be conformed to the image of Christ who is the full expression of God and the vision of what it means to be fully human.

Setting the Captives Free!

In Luke 4:18-19, Jesus began his mission with a message of justice. The passage itself is a quote from Isaiah 61:1-2 and refers to the restoration of the people of Israel. The deeper significance in the ministry of Jesus is that he identified freedom as the fulfilment of his ministry. Certainly, it means freedom from sin in the life of the individual, but it is more than that. The passage refers to the Year of Jubilee, an Old Testament law requiring that every 50 years all debts be cancelled, and all land returned to its traditional title holders. Using this reference to Jubilee indicates that the salvation that Jesus brought involves significant renewal at every level including economic, environmental, and social; it is a wholistic vision of salvation. This is good news!

God's freedom breaks the cycle of violence that sees oppressed become oppressor as regimes are toppled and power shifts occur. The community established at Mount Sinai was reminded that God required justice toward the foreigner in their midst *because* of the liberation from bondage Israel had just experienced. The way of the kingdom of God is to refuse domination, exclusion, and violence. Mission that is shaped by the cross of Christ reorders loyalties and relationships. Priorities change as power is used for the benefit of others, and resources are not horded to the detriment of the needy.[51] This is a powerful expression of justice that reflects the redeeming life of the triune God in the midst of the community.

Ministry of Reconciliation

The ministry of reconciliation is central to the fulfilment of the mission of God. It is the manifestation of justice as seen in Romans 5:10-11. As former enemies, Paul said we have now been reconciled to God through the death of Christ. But the reconciliation that Paul preached was more than a mysterious forgetting of past wrongs against God. In 2 Corinthians 5:17-18 he proclaimed that reconciliation made new creation. And furthermore, the recipients of reconciliation now became agents of reconciliation. In Christ *both* the victim of injustice and the perpetrator become "new creation." This reality is an absurdity to a world embroiled in power politics and dominance, but in the kingdom of God forgiveness creates space for this new reality. It is not simply a return to the status quo that existed before, but the establishment of relationship that overcomes the ancient roots of disunity. However, reconciliation is incomplete until the whole universe is reconciled in Christ, and God is all in all. None are excluded from this process. Practices that advance this process of reconciliation are *healing, truth-telling, the pursuit of justice* and *forgiveness.*[52]

Reconciliation and justice flow in four relational directions. First, vertically between humanity and God. God takes the initiative and invites people in the power of this reconciliation to partner in the process. Second, there is an internal flow of reconciliation needed within each person. This is reconciliation of who we are with who we ought to be, a coming to terms with brokenness and a receiving of God's healing. The third is a horizontal flow that brings reconciliation between "neighbours." In a world wreaked with conflict and fear, reconciling broken relationships between individuals, within families and communities, and even between nations, is vital. The fourth directional flow of reconciliation is the desperate need for humanity to be reconciled to its relationship with the environment.

Wesley stated that the mission of the church is "first, to save each his own soul; then to assist each other in working out their salvation; and afterwards, as far as in them lies, to save all [people] from present and future misery, to overturn the kingdom of Satan, and to set up the Kingdom of Christ."[53] The mission of the church is none other than to spread scriptural holiness throughout the world. Scriptural holiness speaks of authentic spirituality that is rooted in a complete surrender to and love for God and results in an expression of love for neighbour, which seeks the well-being of all people. It is a mission that grows out of an experience of the transforming love of God in Christ, which then works to embody what the Spirit is doing to bring to fulness the creative-redemptive purposes of God.

DISCUSSION QUESTIONS

1. What "works of the devil" (or injustices) do you recognise in our society? In the Gospels, how does Jesus model "destroying" these works? How can your church follow Jesus in this regard?

2. In Richard Niebuhr's description of the relationship between "Christ and culture," where does the ministry of your church fit? Which of these five approaches do you hold and why?

3. How can you apply the ideas of the "four relational directions" of reconciliation in your community? How are these best communicated in your cultural context?

CHAPTER 8

MISSION AND HOLINESS

For some people holiness is a judgemental attitude towards others (e.g., I am holier than you). For others it is regarded as a level of spirituality that is only attainable by an enlightened elite. Holiness is seldom expected to be found beyond the walls of the monastery, let alone in the busy market streets or in the work place. Yet, to separate the idea of holiness from the social dimension of life is to unravel a deeply intertwined aspect of what it means to be human. Modern secular society fails to provide satisfying answers to the fundamental issues of human existence and meaning. It fails to provide an adequate framework for dealing with death and tragedy, obligation and love.[54] True holiness teaches lessons of humility and care, which are basic to being human because it draws from the revelation of the Creator to shape identity and purpose.

"Holiness is active love to God and neighbour based on God's prior love poured into the heart; happiness is the enjoyment and security in such love."[55] Understanding holiness in this relational way locates it at the heart of human community. The primary relationship is of response to God's initiative of love. This response is never isolated since encounter with God inevitably propels a person toward mission, which is an invitation to others to join in the experience of the life of God in the soul.

When the church lives out its intended purpose in society, it becomes a place of transformation. As the Holy Spirit works through the church and the shared lives of its members, it becomes a witness that the reign of

God has already begun in our world. Where this reality is tangible, and holiness is reintegrated into the fabric of social being, the church ceases to need an evangelistic strategy because "the church *is* the evangelistic strategy."[56]

Holiness Creates Community

To understand the strategy of God's mission through the church, it is necessary to examine the biblical, missional community. The encounter with the God who delivers the people from bondage forms a community set apart for God's redemptive purposes.[57] Starting with the formation of the people of Israel in the Exodus, through to the birth of the church at Pentecost, worship acts as the "primal response to God's gracious act of deliverance, and the creative centre of life as a community of faith."[58] Through their worship, God's deliverance is remembered and re-enacted. Furthermore, worship shapes the life of the community by drawing them to participate in the holiness of God (Leviticus 19:1-2). There is a truth in the statement that says, "You become what you worship."

Worship, in the biblical community, is not a passive expression of devotion to God. It is an enactment of God's holiness manifested practically as *righteousness.* In this context it is not a feeling of pure goodness, but a way of interacting with others to ensure that everyone in the community is treated justly. In order to be life giving, righteous living must be infused with compassion lest it become self-righteous. The community shaped by conforming to and expressing God's holiness is propelled into the purpose of God to restore wholeness and fulness to creation.

Practical Holiness

One of the earliest expressions of what a community of holiness should look like is found in the book of Leviticus. Known as the Holiness Code, it defined for Israel what it meant to be a holy nation. Surprisingly, in the climactic chapter of this code, holiness was not defined by rituals or devotional practices, but rather by ways of displaying honesty, kindness, compassion, and justice to others. This understanding of holiness derives from a unique understanding of God's character. In Leviticus 19 the people were called to replicate God's holiness (verse 2) in practical expressions of love toward neighbour (verse 18) *and* foreigner (verse 34). Love in this context should be understood as faithfulness—faithful to represent the character of God in community, and faithful to spread the knowledge of God to the ends of the earth. It is from this character of faithful love that mission flows in order to draw all life back into community with the Source.

The identity of early Israel was not formed by shared history or purpose, but by how they were called to treat each other. Their social interactions reflected their understanding of who they were in relation to God, and holiness was perceived not as an individual privilege but a communal necessity. Far from being totally "other worldly," holiness has direct bearing on how people live their lives together. The basis of these social standards is the call to holiness issued by the holy God. It is important to note that the call to holiness is issued to the whole community, and then God defines how persons in the community are to interact with each other. While many withdraw from social life to seek holiness, the picture of holiness in Leviticus is developed through social interaction. Christian confusion over the understanding of Leviticus is located in a misunderstanding of the communal nature of its vision. This communal emphasis contrasts the emphasis on the individual apparent in much of contemporary Christian thought.

While the Bible calls God holy, it does not explain what God's holiness is in itself. To the biblical mind, however, "The Living God" is not simply an abstract concept, but an experienced reality of God's actions in and through the community. Israel's self-awareness as God's "holy people" in the midst of the cultural milieu of the day called for a lifestyle that was distinct. The Covenant between God and Israel marked the boundary of the community, and inclusion within the boundary was contingent on covenantal faithfulness.[59] Similarly, the church exists within the world and must necessarily establish a distinction between itself and the world. In an effort to contextualise the gospel, care needs to be exercised to uphold the identity of a holy community shaped by Christ.

Wesley was careful to qualify what he meant by holiness by using the term *Christian perfection*. This term has been misunderstood to imply some kind of claim to sinless perfection or fortified moral high ground. Plainly stated, Wesley said: "we expect to be made perfect in love."[60] It is in this relational distinction that Wesley draws attention to the heart of the matter. It is God's love in us that is perfected by receiving and sharing that love with others. There is no absolute perfection this side of the grave, and no approximation of perfection. There is always the possibility for increase in knowing and loving God.[61]

Within this context, the holy community is the expression of the mission of God, and should never be insular. Dietrich Bonhoeffer reminds us that "Those who love their dream of a Christian community more than the Christian community itself become destroyers of that Christian community even though their personal intentions may be ever so honest, earnest, and sacrificial."[62] Individuals in the community are working out their salvation and even mature Christians may need to deal with the consequences of weak and limited understanding. This is not an excuse for sin, but a recognition that the manner in which members of the holy community deal with each other at these points of imperfection demonstrates the extent of God's redeeming love at work in the community.

Three-Dimensional Holiness

Abstract concepts of holiness do little to impact either individual or community. Israel's missional holiness was manifest in three key aspects: spirituality, institution, and ethics. These three dimensions interlocked to construct a tangible expression of holiness.

The Spiritual Dimension. God's presence is often communicated to humanity through the image of light, fire, or smoke. The invisible is made visible and the intangible is experienced. These spiritual experiences are beyond rational analysis, and often those who experience God in this way struggle to describe their experience. The spiritual dimension of holiness creates wonder and awe, and often generates intense emotional responses—a sense of being overwhelmed by the presence of God.

In isolation, the spiritual dimension of holiness has little practical relevance to the wider world and is highly subjective and individualistic.

Israel's understanding of God's holiness was primarily in terms of transcendence, exaltedness, and otherness.[63] This testifies to God's otherworldliness; God is not part of the created order in any way, but stands above it as creator, unlike the gods of the ancient Near East who were believed to be materially part of creation. God is described in the Old Testament as unique, with no comparison or equal: "Who among the gods is like you, LORD? Who is like you—majestic in holiness, awesome in glory, working wonders?" (Exodus 15:11).   At Sinai, the holiness of God was manifest in a spectacular show of light and glory. Five key elements of this spiritual encounter of holiness have been identified as: (1) awe inspiring; (2) unapproachably overpowering majesty; (3) energising; (4) wholly other; and (5) compelling and spiritually intoxicating.[64] This image of an awesome, majestic, and mysteriously holy God is fundamentally connected to Israel's experience of salvation. It seared an enduring image of who God was on the imagination and mind of the biblical community.

While the spiritual dimension of holiness described Israel's experience of God, it was not isolated from practical life. To make sense of the spiritual and to respond appropriately, a second dimension or expression of holiness developed, namely institutional holiness.

The Institutional, or Religious Dimension. Israel's religious practice of holiness through prescribed rituals reminded the community of their central and centring relationship with God. By positioning their worship space (the tabernacle) in the centre of their camp, and making the Sabbath the focal point of the week, Israel was constantly reminded of the presence of God shaping their identity. Through ritual cleansing, they were reminded of the need for deeper personal cleansing. Through ritual rites of passage, they were reminded of the deeper journey of life. Objects, people, times, and places were not just dedicated, but dedicated to what was considered good, and kept from what was associated with evil.[65]

Their society was organised around their understanding of God's nature and an appropriate response to that understanding. Religious holiness dramatised this understanding through ritual and ceremony. Even Israel's dietary regulations served this purpose. Holiness was equated to order and what is proper. Rules demarcating clean and unclean were not so much doctrinal as they were discipline. That which did not conform to what was considered the norm was declared unclean, while that which fulfilled its perceived place in the created order was deemed clean. The issue at stake was life and respect in the community, not the intrinsic value of the nature of the objects or animals in question.[66] Holiness reflected the order and discipline seen in God's creation of structure and discipline out of the formless void that existed in the beginning (see Genesis 1:2).

Organising and regulating life in this way led the community members to explore the nature of God at each turn of the day. This ritualistic holiness established rhythms in everyday life that enhanced the total meaning of life. Everything had its place and meaning, and all was connected to the Creator of life. The experience of life was enhanced as people discovered and fulfilled their roles within such a communal context.

The Ethical Dimension of Holiness. For some the religious dimension of holiness, with its external rules and rituals is often the most prominent concept of holiness, and often considered onerous and burdensome. But it would be a mistake to equate the Holiness Code of Leviticus with simple ritualism with no reference to any ethical content. The call to integrate holiness into every aspect of life was born at Mount Sinai and grew through the Old Testament prophets and on into the New Testament response to God. Ethical holiness was fused to the spiritual and institutional dimensions in a way addressing the whole person. The ethical was embedded in the spiritual, not so it would become more spiritual, but so that the spiritual might engage with the realities of life and envelop the way people lived and interacted with each other so that the image of God would be seen in human community.

Even the dietary laws of the Old Testament contained an ethical ingredient. The prohibition against eating predatory animals may have reflected a teaching that violence was not a part of God's created order, and should not become part of a holy people, even in what they consumed.[67] In the law given to Israel, God demonstrated an ethical character, and it did not take much imagination to conclude that God's call to holiness was a call to the same ethical behaviour. God's faithfulness to Israel as deliverer and saviour was emulated in their faithfulness to maintaining ethical holiness in the community, bringing to fulfilment in their daily living what God started by liberating them from oppression. God was not just a mysterious force, but Divine Being who reacted against and responded to injustice and oppression, and this becomes the standard of righteousness for the community.

The moral values revealed in the Ten Commandments, and the call to holiness in Leviticus 19 indicated an ethical understanding of the Law and of holiness. It was not intended to only govern religion, but to transform every aspect of society. This was not just for the life of Israel; they were called to be a light to the nations and a model of a humane society governed by the principle of life and blessing drawn from a knowledge and experience of God the Creator.

DISCUSSION QUESTIONS

1. What common misconception of holiness have you encountered? How does holiness and mission relate in your community?

2. In what ways could holiness build community in your culture?

3. How is the mission of God expressed in your church? How do the three dimensions of holiness operate to give a practical picture of holiness?

CHAPTER 9

CONCLUSION

John Wesley's call to "spread scriptural holiness throughout the land" conceives of mission that not only offers forgiveness of sin, but more significantly proclaims God's liberation from the power of sin and the hope of transformation through the work of the Holy Spirit. This vision of a holiness mission is not perceived as the idle pursuit of a religious elite, but the formation of a holy people, "whose life is characterised by 'justice, mercy and truth.'"[68] It is not the spreading of moralistic rules and legalism, but the spreading of the life of God embodied in real people. It works to establish communities of authenticity that embrace Christlike holiness as a way of living out God's creational intentions through the empowerment of the Holy Spirit.

Philippians 2:6-11 describes the mission of Jesus. He emptied himself and was born in human likeness; he humbled himself and became obedient even to the point of death. Jesus is the example of a holy life—one fully surrendered to God. In his emptying, Jesus embodied God in this world. Every Christmas the world affirms Jesus as Emmanuel—GOD WITH US. This is more than a fancy theological doctrine; it is an affirmation that Jesus makes God real to us.

When Jesus called his disciples to follow him, it was a call to be with him and to be one with him (John 17:20). Their mission, like ours was to make God known to the world, as Jesus made God known to the world (John 17:25-26). "The New Testament suggests that mission is accomplished by embodying the gospel, as much as by proclaiming it by mouth—and embodying it requires a physical presence."[69] As agents of the gospel, the holy people of God represent the physical presence of God in this world. The mission of holiness is as much to *be* as it is to *do*. "Holiness is never a way out of the world but ever and always a way into the world. It is for the world that the church is called to be both in the world and visibly different from the world."[70] The church is called and sent in order to call and send.

Most people are not initially attracted to God because of the church's doctrines. Instead, they are impacted by the lives of holy people and thus drawn to the holy God displayed. Hebrews 12:14 states, "Make every effort to live in peace with everyone and to be holy; without holiness no one will see the Lord." How will people see the Lord if the church does not embody God's holiness?

The mission of the church is the mission of God, which is to bring to fulness the creative-redemptive purpose of God. There are many books written on mission strategies and methods, but the message should always shape the method. The message of the church is Jesus. Mission offers the world a paradigm of being that is transformative at its core. The mission is rooted in holiness, which is becoming like Christ who is the image of God and calls us to share in this imago Dei. Wesley maintained that "the holy lives of the Christians will be an argument [unbelievers] will not know how to resist."[71]

DISCUSSION QUESTIONS

1. How are you able to enter into the mission of God as demonstrated by Jesus in the Gospels?

2. What are three concepts from this book that you think could strengthen the mission of your church? What are three practical steps you can take to begin implementing these concepts in your life and in your local church?

SUGGESTIONS FOR FURTHER STUDY

Beginner:

Elmer, Duane. *Cross-Cultural Servanthood: Serving the World in Christlike Humility*. Downers Grove: IVP Books, 2006.

Hooker, Morna. *Holiness and Mission: Learning from the Early Church about Mission in the City*. London: SCM Press, 2010.

Horton, Michael. *The Gospel Commission: Recovering God's Strategy for Making Disciples*. Grand Rapids: Baker Books, 2012.

Johnson, Andy. *Holiness and the Missio Dei*. Eugene: Cascade Books, 2016.

Lingenfelter, Sherwood G., and Marvin Keene Mayers. *Ministering Cross-Culturally: A Model for Effective Personal Relationships*. Grand Rapids: Baker Academic, 2016.

Tucker, Frank. *Intercultural Communication for Christian Ministry*. Adelaide, Australia: Frank Tucker, 2007.

Intermediate to Advanced:

Akkerman, Jay Richard, and Mark A. Maddix. *Missional Discipleship: Partners in God's Redemptive Mission*. Kansas City: Beacon Hill Press, 2013.

Bosch, David J. *Transforming Mission - Paradigm Shifts in Theology of Mission*. Maryknoll: Orbis Books, 2011.

Davis, C. A. *Making Disciples Across Cultures: Missional Principles for a Diverse World*. Downers Grove: IVP Books, 2015.

Flemming, Dean E. *Recovering the Full Mission of God: A Biblical Perspective on Being, Doing and Telling*. IVP Academic, 2013.

Hessalgrave, D. J. *Communicating Christ Cross Culturally.* Grand Rapids, Michigan: Zondervan, 1991.

Hiebert, P.G. *Transforming Worldviews: An Anthropological Understanding of How People Change.* Grand Rapids: Baker Academic, 2008.

Muck, Terry. *Christianity encountering world religions: the practice of mission in the twenty-first century.* Grand Rapids: Baker Academic, 2009.

Schwanz, Keith, and Joseph E. Coleson. *Missio Dei: A Wesleyan Understanding.* Kansas City,: Beacon Hill Press, 2011.

Tennent, Timothy C. *Theology in the Context of World Christianity: How the Global Church is influencing the Way We think about and Discuss Theology.* Grand Rapids: Zondervan, 2007.

Wright, Christopher J. H. *The Mission of God: Unlocking the Bible's Grand Narrative.* Downers Grove: IVP Academic, 2006.

NOTES

1   David J. Bosch, *Transforming Mission: Paradigm Shifts in Theology of Mission* (Maryknoll: Orbis, 1991), 5.
2   Lesslie Newbigin, *The Open Secret: An Introduction to the Theory of Mission* (Grand Rapids: Eerdmans, 1995), 29.
3   C. S. Lewis, "The Four Loves: Charity," found at https://renovare.org/articles/the-four-loves-charity, accessed December 12, 2017.
4   Christopher J. H. Wright, *The Mission of God: Unlocking the Bible's Grand Narrative* (Downers Grove: IVP Academic), 29.
5   Wright, *The Mission of God*, 31.
6   Dean E. Flemming, *Recovering the Full Mission of God: A Biblical Perspective on Being, Doing and Telling* (Downers Grove: IVP Academic, 2013), 28.
7   Bosch, *Transforming Mission*, 10.
8   Bosch, *Transforming Mission*, 11.
9   Roger Peterson, "Missio Dei or 'Missio Me'? Using Short-Term Missions to Contribute Toward the Fulfilment of God's Global Purpose," found at http://www.soe.org/explore/wp-content/uploads/2011/10/Perspectives_Chpt_134.pdf, accessed November 12, 2017.
10 Peterson, "Missio Dei or 'Missio Me'?".
11 James W. Sire, *The Universe Next Door: A Basic Worldview Catalogue* (Downers Grove: InterVarsity, 2009), 20.
12 Sire, *The Universe Next Door*, 22-23.
13 James Engel. "The Road to Conversion, The Latest Research," *Evangelical Missions Quarterly* 26. 2 (1990): 184-193.
14 James F. Engel and William A. Dyrness. *Changing the Mind of Missions: Where Have We Gone Wrong?* (Downers Grove: InterVarsity, 2000), 101.
15 Bryan P. Stone, *Evangelism After Christendom: The Theology and Practice of Christian Witness* (Grand Rapids: Brazos, 2007), 257.
16 Paul G. Hiebert, *Cultural Anthropology*, 2nd ed. (Grand Rapids: Baker, 1983), 177.
17 Charles R. Gailey and Howard Culbertson, *Discovering Missions* (Kansas City: Beacon Hill, 2007), 14.
18 Geert Hofstede, *Culture's Consequences: International Differences in Work-Related Values* (Newbury Park: Sage, 1980), 25.
19 Figure 3 is adapted from: Paul G. Hiebert, Transforming Worldview: An Anthropological Understanding of How People Change (Grand Rapids: Baker Academic, 2009), 26.
20 Kenneth Scott Latourette, *A History of Christian Mission in China* (Piscataway: Gorgias, 2009), 382.

21 Soon Ang and Linn Van Dyne, *Handbook of Cultural Intelligence* (Hoboken: Taylor and Francis, 2015), 3.
22 Ang and Van Dyne, *Cultural Intelligence,* 3-10.
23 Duane Elmer, *Cross-Cultural Servanthood: Serving the World in Christlike Humility* (Downers Grove: IVP, 2006), 39.
24 John R. Baldwin, et al., *Intercultural Communication for Everyday Life* (Hoboken: John Wiley & Sons, 2013), 250-251.
25 Dennis Bratcher, "Speaking the Language of Canaan: The Old Testament and the Israelite Perception of the Physical World. How the Scriptures Appropriate Non-Hebraic World Views," found at http://www.crivoice.org/langcaan.html, accessed December 14, 2017.
26 Henry H. Knight and F. Douglas Powe, *Transforming Evangelism: The Wesleyan Way of Sharing Faith* (Nashville: Discipleship Resources, 2006), 45.
27 Albert Mehrabian, "'Silent Messages'—A Wealth of Information About Nonverbal Communication (Body Language)," found at http://www.kaaj.com/psych/smorder.html, accessed December 14, 2017).
28 Elmer, *Cross-Cultural Servanthood,* 82.
29 Adapted from David J. Hesselgrave, *Communicating Christ Cross Culturally* (Grand Rapids: Zondervan, 1991), 163-168.
30 Rachel Adelson, "Hue and Views: A cross-cultural study reveals how language shapes color perception." *Monitor on Psychology* 36.2 (2005): 26, found at http://www.apa.org/monitor/feb05/hues.aspx, accessed December 20, 2017.
31 Marshall McLuhan, "The Medium is the Message," found at http://web.mit.edu/allanmc/www/mcluhan.mediummessage.pdf, accessed December 20, 2017.
32 Wright, *The Mission of God,* 63.
33 Stone, *Evangelism after Christendom,* 15.
34 Stone, *Evangelism after Christendom,* 175-221.
35 Andrew C. Thompson, "From Societies to Society: The Shift from Holiness to Justice in the Wesleyan Tradition," *Methodist Review 3* (2011): 162.
36 Thompson, "From Societies to Society," 163.
37 Knight and Powe, *Transforming Evangelism,* 79.
38 Elmer, *Cross-Cultural Servanthood,* 146.
39 Adapted from Elmer, *Cross-cultural Servanthood,* 142.
40 Newbigin, *The Open Secret,* 134.
41 John Travis (a pseudonym), "The C1 to C6 Spectrum: A Practical Tool for Defining Six Types of 'Christ-centered Communities' ('C') Found in the Muslim Context," *Evangelical Missions Quarterly* 34.4 (1998): 407-408.
42 "Minutes of Several Conversations between the Reverend Mr. John and Charles Wesley, and Others" in *The Works of John Wesley Volume 10: The Methodist Societies, the Minutes of Conference*, ed. by Henry D. Rack (Nashville: Abingdon, 2011), 845.
43 Ken Wytsma. *Pursuing Justice: The Call to Live and Die for Bigger Things* (Nashville: Thomas Nelson, 2013), 7.
44 David N. Field "Holiness, Social Justice and the Mission of the Church: John Wesley's Insights in Contemporary Context." *Holiness: The Journal of Wesley House Cambridge* 1.2 (2015): 181.
45 Flemming, *Recovering the Full Mission of God,* 34.

46 Paul D. Hanson, *The People Called: The Growth of Community in the Bible* (Louisville: Westminster John Knox, 2002), 41.

47 Hanson, *The People Called,* 46.

48 Richard Niebuhr, *Christ and Culture* (New York: Harper, 1951).

49 Scot McKnight, *Kingdom Conspiracy: Returning to the Radical Mission of the Local Church* (Grand Rapids: Baker, 2016), 94.

50 McKnight, *Kingdom Conspiracy,* 95-96.

51 Stone, *Evangelism after Christendom,* 177.

52 Robert Schreiter, "Mission as a Ministry of Reconciliation?" *Norsk Tidsskrift For Misjonsvitenskap* 2 (2013): 76, found at http://www.egede.no/sites/default/files/dokumenter/pdf/Schreiter%202-2013.pdf, accessed November 29, 2017.

53 John Wesley, "The Reformation of Manners," found at http://wesley.nnu.edu/john-wesley/the-sermons-of-john-wesley-1872-edition/sermon-52-the-reformation-of-manners/, accessed November 27, 2017.

54 Hanson, *The People Called,* 8.

55 David B. McEwan, "Love, Holiness and Happiness: The Wesleyan Prescription for Effective Mission," *Crucible* 6.2 (2015): 3, found at http://www.crucibleonline.net/wp-content/uploads/2016/08/McEwan-Love-Holiness-and-Happiness-Crucible-6-2-May-2015.pdf, accessed November 10, 2017.

56 Stone, *Evangelism after Christendom,* 16.

57 Hanson, *The People Called,* 69.

58 Hanson, *The People Called,* 41.

59 Gordon J. Wenham, *The Book of Leviticus,* The New International Commentary on the Old Testament (Grand Rapids: Eerdmans, 1979), 22-32.

60 John Wesley, "Satan's Devices," found at http://wesley.nnu.edu/john-wesley/the-sermons-of-john-wesley-1872-edition/sermon-42-satans-devices/, accessed December 5, 2017.

61 David B. McEwan, *The Life of God in the Soul: The Integration of Love, Holiness, and Happiness in the Thought of John Wesley* (Milton Keynes: Paternoster, 2015), 59.

62 Bonhoeffer cited in McKnight, *Kingdom Conspiracy,* 40.

63 John G. Gamme, *Holiness in Israel* (Minneapolis: Fortress, 1989), 4.

64 Rudolph Otto cited in Gamme, *Holiness in Israel,* 5.

65 Jackie A. Naudé, "7727" *New International Dictionary of Old Testament Theology and Exegesis,* vol 3, ed. Willem A. Van Gemeran (Grand Rapids: Zondervan, 1997), 885.

66 Mary Douglas, "The Abominations of Leviticus", reprinted in Bernhard Lang (ed.), *Anthropological Approaches to the Old Testament* (Philadelphia: Fortress, 1985), 103-108.

67 Gamme, *Holiness in Israel,* 11.

68 Field, *Holiness, Social Justice and the Mission of the Church,* 190.

69 Morna Hooker, *Holiness and Mission: Learning from the Early Church about Mission in the City,* (London: SCM, 2010), Kindle location 930-932.

70 Stone, *Evangelism after Christendom,* 191.

71 John Wesley's sermon "The General Spread of the Gospel," found at http://wesley.nnu.edu/john-wesley/the-sermons-of-john-wesley-1872-edition/sermon-63-the-general-spread-of-the-gospel/, accessed December 16, 2017.

FRAMEWORKS FOR LAY LEADERSHIP

ABOUT THE EDITOR

Rob A. Fringer, PhD–Principal and lecturer in Biblical Studies and Biblical Language at Nazarene Theological College in Brisbane. Rob is an ordained elder in the Church of the Nazarene and has 15 years of pastoral experience working in the areas of Youth, Adult Discipleship, and Community Outreach. He is co-author of *Theology of Luck: Fate, Chaos, & Faith* and *The Samaritan Project* both published by Beacon Hill Press of Kansas City. Rob is married (Vanessa) and has two children (Sierra and Brenden).

BOOKS IN THE
FRAMEWORKS FOR LAY LEADERSHIP SERIES

ENGAGING THE STORY OF GOD
Rob A. Fringer

EXPLORING A WESLEYAN THEOLOGY
David B. McEwan

EMBODYING A THEOLOGY OF MINISTRY AND LEADERSHIP
Bruce G. Allder

ENTERING THE MISSION OF GOD
Richard Giesken

EXPRESSING A NAZARENE IDENTITY
Floyd Cunningham

EMBRACING A DOCTRINE OF HOLINESS
David B. McEwan and Rob A. Fringer

www.ingramcontent.com/pod-product-compliance
Lightning Source LLC
Chambersburg PA
CBHW021139020426
42331CB00005B/829